AF191420

A true story about fear, hope, healing and freedom

NO EMOTIONS ALLOWED

Ewa Babicka

novum pro

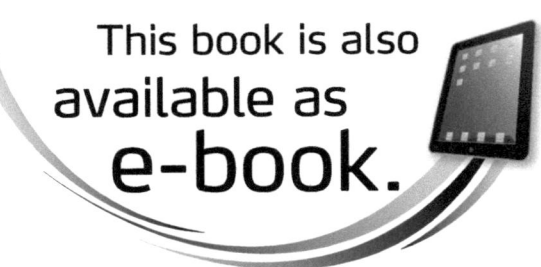

www.novum-publishing.co.uk

© 2024 novum publishing

ISBN 978-3-99146-225-5
Editing: Chris Beale
Cover photos: Roman Prysiazhniuk, Molotok007 I Dreamstime.com
Cover design, layout & typesetting: novum publishing

www.novum-publishing.co.uk

Print product with financial
climate contribution
ClimatePartner.com/16547-2311-1001

Contents

Preface

This book was growing within me for a long time with a speed and force of a hurricane at some points. My emotions, feelings and countless thoughts were boiling inside me during all these events and situations which I'm going to share with you here. All this in general was a result of forced labour as an illegal worker which I was experiencing at the time. Unfortunately, even today there are still many victims of that vicious procedure all over the world.

It will take you through the journey of life of legal and illegal migrants in the Republic of Ireland (ROI) not long ago. You will find here a real story about forced labour, discrimination, prejudice. I will expose challenges that most immigrants were facing on a daily basis on many levels. Language barriers, cultural diversity, physical exploitation, mental exhaustion, lack of certainty and support. All of them mixed with emotions of fear and hopes for the best. It is an explosive cocktail!

It is not my intention to scare you at the beginning. These are real stories. Some were fun with unexpected twists and happy endings, and some were sad, tragic. Some of the stories here are only to reflect on particular events. Some are warnings, because for many immigrants similar stories are still real and ongoing. My intention is to raise awareness of modern slavery forced labour of non-trafficked individuals that is still real, here and now. My intention is to "break the silence" of shameful exploitation that happens in developed countries, not in the "third world".

Nevertheless, those stories are based on real events, names are changed for obvious reasons and any similarities are only random, not intentional. In real life, anything can happen with or without any warnings. Same here, expect the unexpected or do not expect anything and just enjoy reading.

This book is also about personal transformation.

Here is a collection of real stories that changed ME! I am sharing with you my personal path at the beginning of my personal transformation. It was a difficult way, packed with bumps, ups and downs, surprises, and some really unpleasant events. Many would say: *"What doesn't kill you, makes you stronger."*[1] Sounds great, but we are not here in this life to suffer, struggle and fight for the joyful life we all deserve. In my personal, humble opinion we are here to create our meaningful, happy life.

You might agree, you might not. It's an individual approach and I entirely respect that. Although sometimes we need someone to tell us to slow down, to step back, look at the bigger picture and reflect on our situation, asking: *"What else can I do here? How can I make things different to get better results, to improve my life and be happy?"*

Here I am sharing with you my real experience, thoughts, emotions, and tools that helped me to get through personal transformation. At the end of each chapter you will find a section called 'Your Daily Exercises'. This is where you find tools and instructions helping you to practice positive thinking, positive affirmations, visualisations and assertive skills. There are also exercises for breathing and calming techniques invented by other practitioners, and introductions to mindfulness and meditation exercises.

The full collection of tools with instructions you will find in the last part of this book – Your Daily Exercises. I can quickly and honestly answer three questions: *"Was it easy?" NO! "Did it happen overnight?" NO! "Was it worth it?" YES! YES! YES!*

In this book, I am taking you on an "everything is possible" journey, all this to improve your life. First accept that *Perfection* does not exist! But you can try to do good or better next time. Second, you are not failure, you are learner. Third, stop comparing yourself to anybody else. It's your life, not others. Fourth,

---

1 Nietzsche.

drop the guilt and "I should" *monkeys*. There is nothing selfish in caring about yourself, your needs, your emotions, your well-being. Finally, accept yourself for who you are, you are imperfectly perfect, you are enough, you are worthy.

My goal is to encourage you to start thinking positively about yourself, to love yourself infinitely, and to see your life in a different light. To be curious, to seek other options and be open to opportunities for a happier life! Yes! To change *"impossible"* into *POSSIBLE!*

Of course, I cannot promise anything, neither changes nor miracles. It is entirely up to you if you want that change. But I hope that this book will give you "food for thought".

So, take your time, check out the tools described here. Give them a try and gain new perspective regarding Yourself and Your life.

Most importantly, have fun and enjoy the journey!

Disclaimer

This book is a memoir. It reflects the author's present recollections of experiences over time. Some names and characters have been changed, some events have been compressed, and some dialogue has been recreated.

CHAPTER 1

THE BROKEN HEART GOES TO THE GREEN ISLAND

What is the connection? My heart was broken into so many pieces by a long-term so called "partner" that even a hoover would struggle to collect all of them. The "individual" was unable to cut off his mummy who hated me deeply. I fought for six years, but I had to give up and let her keep her boy. Maybe, if I were wealthy and from a prestigious family, she would let go of her passive aggression and possessiveness. But no, I was not good enough for her boy. Full stop.

Consequently, his love declarations were shallow and faded with time. To the extent of having an affair with a friend of our friend. It was devastating, humiliating and crossed all boundaries. My broken heart couldn't take any more. Whose heart would? We give so much of our life, energy, emotions, empathy, engagement, attention to so many people. Many of them do not even deserve to be looked at. This is a topic for a separate chapter.

Anyway, my broken heart and relationship were not enough! If something is going badly in one department of my life, you can bet all the crap will be set loose simultaneously in other departments too.

On top of that, the company I was working for also disappeared into thin air. Literally! One day I was working in a big office and dealt with four bosses. Next day, the bosses moved back to the other side of the country and stopped taking my calls. I was running the whole business without them until the money stopped coming in. Including my wages!

Has anyone tried to make a living without money? Yeah, of course! Has anyone tried for five months? Oh, not so many! One would say: "Go and get another job!" Yes, of course, it crossed my mind, believe me! However, not at the time in my country, and for many other reasons. I was still a contracted employee even without a boss around. Nightmare! Only jobs on the "black market" were available, cash in hand, no insurance, no guaranteed hours. Fair enough, I did some odd jobs out of desperation; I can do all DIY jobs, home or office make over. Anything but electricity!

Then, a call from a friend of our family came. An absolutely random call, as we were not so close. He was always somewhere abroad.

"Hello! It's me, Frank!" said the voice I knew.

"Hello, Frank! Long-time no hear from you? Where are you now? States? Canada? Australia?" I tried to guess his location. He travelled a lot.

"Oh, no, not that far. I am in the Republic of Ireland," Frank said.

"Fantastic! What are you doing there? Are you with your family?" I was curious, but I knew that he preferred to travel on his own.

"No, just me and some friends. I work in a local company. It is a small village, peace, quiet, good money," Frank explained.

"WOW! This is what I am looking for now. I am serious!" I said it calmly but inside I was screaming: *"Get me out of here, now, please!"* I was holding my breath and pushed the shout inside.

"Well, I can check a few places here for you. Would you like to come here for long?" Frank asked.

"Would I like to come? I am already packing my 'crap' in my head. I am already at the airport!" I was well ahead of myself.

"I can do many things, you know." I said this as calmly as possible, despite the massive urge to scream and jump like a happy four year old.

"Let me see what is available. I will keep you posted. How are things at your end?" Frank asked.

"Well, so many things happened and changed that it will take me a month to tell you about it. Maybe next time when we have a chance to talk face to face?" I was still visualising my trip to ROI in my head.

"Other than that, we are all alive," I summarised because I was unable to put a single sentence together. My mind was drifting far away, on its way to ROI.

My mother took the receiver and continued a friendly chat with Frank.

"WOW, what's just happened? Is it real? Have I been rescued from the misery of unfortunate events? Believe it or not? What if I can't cope with long distance, language, culture, work?" My thoughts were galloping through my mind.

All possible "what if..." came out within next seconds right after a euphoric vision of me going abroad. THE FEAR! Fear of the unknown.

The next questions came soon after fear. What if it is my chance for a better life, for a future, for love? What holds me here? What else can I do? What choices do I have?

"#FIA – f$%^ it all – I am going, if not to ROI and Frank I will go wherever." I finally convinced myself.

For the next few weeks, I was tiptoeing around the idea.

Managing and arranging many things almost at the same time. I bought a return ticket to Dublin, but the return date had a bit of a twist, a leap of faith I guess. Honestly, I should have played the lottery back then. Damn!

· ·

The Grand day came faster than I expected. I never felt so ready and eager in my life with itchy feet to go anywhere.

Vroom! I am on my way to the airport in Berlin, connecting flight to London Heathrow and from there to Dublin.

The first flight was fine, I landed smoothly at London Heathrow at the gate 11. My connecting flight to Dublin was taking off in 2 hours at the gate 89. *"Easy peasy Japanese. I will have enough time to stop at the smoking room,"* I thought. At the time, smoking was allowed in all social spaces and had the designated areas for it.

Have you ever been to London Heathrow Airport? Well, let me tell you, it is enormous! I was walking with my big suitcase and hand luggage, sweating like a Sumo contestant for an hour to find out that I have just reached gate... 30! And no sign of a smoking area!

What was more, I was walking next to those moving paths where people were swiftly, effortlessly moving forward. *"Phi! Are you all so lazy to walk? A bit of exercise keeps you fit, it doesn't kill you,"* I thought, *but* I was so wrong like never ever in my life.

Then it came to me. *"If I am not going to jump on those moving paths, I am not going to get to gate 89 on time."* I was convincing myself. Not to mention a quick stop for a puff. *"Oh hell NO, I am not going to miss either of those."*

So, I joined the "lazy people" and in a few minutes I reached gates 60 to 70 where smoking areas were assigned. In five big puffs, I "swallowed" the cigarette and jumped again on the moving paths.

It took me one hour and forty-five minutes after my first landing to reach gate 89. The boarding for Dublin began just as I arrived. *"Ooohhh, I was so close to missing it."* I felt relieved and tired, like a horse after the Grand National.

As I relaxed during the relatively short flight, I forgot about instructions given by Frank, which went as follows:

"On arrival in Dublin you will have to fill a residential card with all your and my details. Write down all my details, the address, name of my workplace, contact details. Remember! You are a visitor, only a visitor!" Frank yelled over the phone the day before my flight.

On arrival, I followed other passengers into the emigration posts and joined the queue without even thinking about Frank's instructions. Then some "tickling" came at the back of my mind that I was missing something here. *"What is it?"* I looked at a passenger who was talking to the emigration officer and he was passing some papers. *"Damn, the residential card, &^&%%^."* I said to myself as I recalled Frank's instructions.

I stepped out of the queue and went around the hall to look for the card. I found the card, filled it in and joined another queue like nothing happened.

Only inside, I was shaking like a leaf and swearing but kept myself composed because... the upcoming conversation was in the English language!

FYI – I hadn't spoken English for fourteen years before I arrived in Dublin! Not a single word! NONE! You know that phrase, "If you do not use it, you lose it!" Mhm, that was me at that very moment! My English was stiff and rusty, like the hinge of an old gate. *"It is what it is, kind of a test. Let's see what you can do."* I encouraged myself, still shaking inside.

Even today, I am not quite sure what happened there, but English words were flowing from my mouth, and all went like this:

"Hello, may I have your travelling documents?" asked the emigration officer.

"Hello. Yes, of course." I passed my passport and the residential card.

"What is your reason for coming to Dublin today?" the officer continued.

"I came to visit family," I said with full confidence in my voice.

"Where does your family live?" The officer threw another routine question.

"All details are on this card." I pointed to the residential card and smiled.

"Good, and how long are you going to stay?" the officer continued.

"Just for a few weeks," I answered softly, still smiling.

"Do you have a return ticket?" the officer asked another routine question.

"Yes, of course." I passed my return ticket to him, knowing exactly what would happen next and mentally preparing myself for the worst-case scenario. My heart almost stopped.

"Your return ticket is in three months," the officer said. He had a puzzled expression on his face.

"Oh, no! It's impossible!" I yelled with disbelief in my voice and a matching shocked expression on my face.

"It is possible. Look at that." The officer showed me my return ticket. He was still cool and curiously checking my reactions. I bet it was part of his training and he got a lot of it on a daily basis. *Do you really think that I don't know that? I have bought it; I've paid for it.*" This was running through my head.

"Look, I really don't understand that. I specifically said four weeks! Gosh, what am I going to do now?" I was in full flow. Damn, I deserved an Oscar nomination for acting as dumb as a wooden log. My disbelief and astonished surprise was pushed out by fear. All together; my face, voice, body and soul were screaming: *"Are you fricking kidding me? I have a wrong return date? No way!"*

"I can't stay here this long! I have a business to run and family to look after." I was talking like a machine. I still don't know where all these words came from. I hadn't spoken English for so long that I shouldn't say anything beyond, "Hello, my name is..."

"OK, I understand. Don't worry, I think there is a way to fix it. You can get to the airlines agent and rebook it for the right time. They have an office here at the airport," the officer said calmly. He sounded like he was genuinely concerned about me.

One more note here, at that time, there were no cheap, chartered airlines. Actually, all the airlines at the time had high standards and for obvious reasons (they do not pay me for advertising) I am not going to state the name of that airline.

"Alright, alright, you are right, but I need to get on the other side. Right?" I was almost holding my breath and freaking out inside. I finally shut up!

"Well, yes... so I will give you a four-week tourist visa and you can go to the airline agent here and reschedule your ticket." The officer said it slowly, like he was making sure that I understood every word. He grabbed the stamp, pressed it into my passport, wrote all dates and passed all the paperwork back to me.

I was standing still with my jaw dropped, still speechless. Just frozen! *"Is he really giving this to me?"*

"Hey, you can go now," the officer said and pointed to the exit door. "Go change your ticket and enjoy Ireland," he said with a smile.

"Thank you," I whispered. At the same time, I was screaming inside: *"I am free, I did it, I am in."*

"You're welcome!" The officer was still smiling.

"Thank you!" His "welcome" unfroze my mind and my feet were almost flying, moving toward the exit door.

Frank was waiting at the arrival door, a bit nervous because he didn't know why it was taking so long. I was not aware of the time at all.

"Sweet Pye! It was a miracle!" I exclaimed the moment I saw him. "Damn right, miracle." I was still euphoric, pumped with a high level of adrenaline.

"Let's go. I need to pay for parking. We have over an hour to drive," Frank said with energy.

While we were walking to his car, I told him what happened back at the emigration check point. Frank laughed and looked at me with disbelief.

"What did you say?" he laughed.

I repeated word for word. I still couldn't believe that I did it. *"Should I think about a career in show business?"*

Frank pointed to his car, and I automatically walked up to the right side of the car to get to the passenger seat. Frank stopped walking because he was laughing at me so hard, watching me getting into the car on the driver side.

"Are you going to drive now?" Frank asked still choking on his laugh.

"What?" I was puzzled. I was still in my "high mood" over my great performance on arrival. I was over the moon that I didn't notice the steering wheel on the right side. It is the opposite side to the continental cars.

"Look!" Frank pointed to the steering wheel while packing my bags into the boot.

I looked at the wheel. It still didn't mean anything to me. On the second thought, *"Why the hell is the steering wheel on the passenger side?"* Click! "Oh, this is big! How can you drive it?" I asked and digested the fact at the same time.

"It takes time, but you will get used to it," Frank said like it was no big deal.

"Yeah... maybe, sure. Eeeh, right now it's so awkward." I was processing new reality. *"It will be so much fun to learn about millions of new things at the speed of light. Go with the flow!"*

I moved to the other side and got into the passenger seat. It felt even more awkward sitting there without the steering wheel in front of me.

"OK, let's go." I shook off a bit of awkwardness.

While Frank was driving, the island started to reveal itself with a famous depth of juicy Irish green.

. . . .

After over an hour's drive, we arrived in a tiny village with the Main Street covered with small shops outnumbered by the pubs. The Main Street was a bit too strong of a name for a street shorter than half a mile. It felt comfortable and cosy.

For me, "the Big City Girl", it was space shock. *"How the hell will I fit in here? Hey, woman, open your mind and all senses to the new experience. It is your new path! The roller-coaster just started! Fantastic!"* I had to remind myself.

The whole village was the size of a block back home. Like you will sneeze on the one side of it, and someone will say "Bless You" on the other end. Honestly, you could walk across the village in less than 10 minutes.

Awesome!

In Frank's small, shared accommodation I met a few of his friends. They were waiting to meet me. Oh, yes, the "new arrival" into the village was a huge entertainment to the whole community of migrants living there. Only a few things were missing, posters, flowers, orchestra, and flags!

There was great food, drinks, fantastic stories, and bursts of laughter.

"I couldn't imagine any better stepping into the unknown, into my new life." I was contemplating new surroundings and enjoying the atmosphere of the gathering. I was absorbing it all like a sponge.

Thank you, Universe![2]

. . . .

The Power of visualisation. See it all in your head! Focus your emotions on the beautiful picture of your goal.

Back then I used the power instinctively. I had no idea that something like that existed. However, my intuition had sent me a clear vision of what it was going to look like to travel to ROI and I held on to that vision tightly. I have seen vivid pictures of my travel, of Ireland, of my dreams and goals. I was very excited about the opportunity; my emotions were strong and positive to keep my visualisation on high vibration. Ask yourself now: "What do I want my life to look like?" and release your imagination.

The Power of visualisation will get you to "Get ready to be ready, to be ready, to be ready!"[3] With full focus on your dream, you need to put something into action. Try new things and see what comes out of that. In my case, it was "fake it till you make

---

2 Disclaimer! I have full respect for all religions, beliefs, etc. That includes everyone's individual approaches, faith, beliefs with no offence to anyone. It is my personal choice to believe in power of positive thinking that creates positive emotions, which together give me powerful belief to make things happen. The source of energy, also named as the Universe sends responses to my manifestations (my thoughts). My positive thinking, appreciation of good things, is charged with great, happy emotions. All together this empowers my beliefs that "everything is always working out for me." That's for starters, farther in the book you will find more details about the power of positive thinking.

3 Abraham Hicks – check her on YouTube.

it!" Stop thinking "What if..." because it will block you before you even start. You will not start because you cannot see and control the outcome! Damn it! Just do it. With every single thought You are creating your future.

Always be grateful for who you are and what you already have. Always say "Thank you for everything and to everyone in my life!"

YOUR DAILY EXERCISES

Today is your first day of loving yourself. The starting point is to pick one exercise and make a commitment to yourself to practice it every day. You are going to learn new skills. Any learning process takes some time, small effort, small steps, and daily repetition. Like learning to walk again. Do you remember how you learnt to walk in the first place? Of course not. You heard stories about your walking adventures from others or watched videos, pictures made at the time, you wouldn't remember that at all. You don't remember your desire to walk. All you wanted was to be able to copy those around you. You started with some stand ups and back on your rump. And again. You were working on your balance, lost it and back on your rump again. You were scared, but you tried step by step. You failed, and you tried again. You have used every opportunity to stand up and shuffle your legs, and back on your rump again. You were curious, you were fearless, you were adventurous. You have used every support available, a carer's hand, furniture, walking toys, even pets. You had joy in doing new things while you heard encouragement to try again. And you did try again, and again. Your reward was coming slowly with fails, bumps and bruises sometimes, but you were unstoppable. You were calm, consistent, focused, and keen to learn new skills. Do you remember that?

I bet you don't remember that, but you are walking now and that's evidence that you are able to learn new skills. Just give yourself a chance to do it again. Instead of waiting for a magic wand to do it instantly, use your own inner power to move towards your happiness.

Stop being a slave of your brain, take control and become the master of your mind. Remember to be positive, consistent, and focus on your self-love.

The Power of visualisation to activate your inner power and imagination

Close your eyes and bring just one picture into your mind related to your dream or goal. Use your imagination and focus on it for one minute. For example: Your dream holiday destination you want to go to. See that place in your head. Where is it? Feel that place as you are there right now. Smell the air in that place. How sweet is the air? Notice the weather. Is it warm, hot, or cold? Notice all the colours around you. Listen to all the sounds around you. Is it quiet, noisy? Do you hear sounds of waves, wind, birds singing, people talking? Do you walk around or just sit in one spot? Feel the excitement of being there. Or do you feel calm, relaxed, safe? Or all together?

Play it all in your mind just for one minute a day. Each time, add more details about that place.

Practice Gratitude

We are taking so many things for granted. By simply saying thank you for everything will help you to stay grounded and notice all things and people in your life. You might be grateful for things like a car, mobile phone, coffee, clothes, bed, home, work, etc. You might be grateful for people in your life: family, friends, children, husband, partner, grandparents, co-workers, teachers. Be grateful for those who are NOT helping you at the moment. They actually do! They are teaching you important lessons. Take it and say thank you.

Most importantly, be grateful for yourself, your body, soul and mind.

CHAPTER 2

THE LAND OF MUSHROOMS

The next few weeks rolled in like a "bullet train", the super-fast train, almost causing dizziness and sickness.

The first thing to fix as quickly as possible was a job. Any job, easy to apply, required basic skills and English language. On my side, I needed to sort out nearby accommodation and transport. The public transport in ROI is still on a basic level. It guarantees an entirely different level of experience when comparing to any other type of transportation in the world. It forced serious questions: *What age are we living in now? What part of the world am I in now?"* Here is a hint: eighteen months passed before I saw a train on that island.

The other thing was the solid habit of driving my own vehicle. Back home I was driving for a living, to me driving was independence and a solid habit. That habit changed rapidly as I couldn't afford a car. I was constantly depending on someone. I didn't complain, though; it wasn't a big deal. Instead, I accepted and took it as an adventure. There was only one negative aspect to those adventures: the weather, the almost notorious rain. Even the Irish make jokes about the weather, like: How many times a week does it rain in Ireland? Twice a week, once for four days, once for three days. Or the island is the only place in the world where it rains from left to right. And so on.

On my arrival, summer decided to visit the island for a few weeks. It was the first hot summer in eight years and the heat of thirty-six degrees Celsius was unbearable for the Irish. It helped me to travel dry and lightly on the country roads, even walking long distance was pleasant.

Nevertheless, I needed a job somewhere near my new home or a job with transport provided or sharing a car with co-workers. The view of my own car was distant and foggy. I was willing to go the extra mile to get a job. *I need to start somewhere, somehow.* I was constantly thinking about it, just one thought over and over. That notorious thought became a wish pretty soon. Although, I didn't say precisely what kind of job I wanted, just a job. So be careful what are you wishing for, because all your thoughts, wishes and emotions WILL become true.

I was so eager and full of energy that I couldn't stand still for a minute. *"Please, give me something to do because I am going 'bananas' here."* Yeah, sitting tight was not my thing at all.

In that sense, the only job available straight away, in the middle of June was... picking mushrooms! *"Are you fricking kidding me? With the IT diploma, advanced office experience, customer service, picking mushrooms? For fifty foxes, really?"* My head was spinning, my heart sank, my positive spirit went down to the damned darkest place. In my mind, I had reached "the bottom" of my existence. What's more, I didn't know that I was heading to the worst workplace; comparable with hell.

Also, I didn't know back then that it was the last part of the previous chapter of my life. Some say that you must reach the bottom of whatever, to feel it under your feet then kick upwards so hard, with enough energy to bring you up to the surface. Like a damn Phoenix from the ashes.

"Hey, take it, make the best of it, and let's see what will happen next. For once in your life, do something for fricking fun. One step at the time." I was giving myself courage and a mental nudge to go with the flow. You Only Live Once - YOLO!

With that YOLO theme, I moved to an even smaller village. The village had a quarter of a mile length of the Main Street, but twelve pubs in total on each side of it. And the one essential shop! *"Wee."*

The detached house I moved into was about a mile outside the village. No immediate neighbours, just fields with cows around. Another *"Wee"* ... for it! The house had six bedrooms, including one master ensuite bedroom and four double bedrooms. Two shared bathrooms with toilets. A huge kitchen with a dining part and the little living room.

Within six of us flatmates, we had four different nationalities. *"Wee…" "multi-culture"* to add some marvellous colours to our co-existence. One couple and three of us in the double rooms and one privileged lady in the master bedroom. The lady was about to return to her country soon and she promised that master room to my roommate on her departure. Although, the master bedroom became a conflict point for two parties, my new roommate and the couple. The rest of us couldn't care less, we were happy to have shelter.

My new roommate was not only the same nationality as me, but was also Frank's close friend. Those alliances put me into a fricking awkward position so many times that it became a burden.

There were times when I wanted to scream, *"Hey, I have enough of my own 'crap', so I don't need yours."* Did I really? The hell, I didn't, so instead I was "chewing" it slowly, and I was "swallowing" the whole drama quietly. Then eventually I'd let it out of my mind by acting absolutely "wild". That "wild" behaviour of mine was simply to work like a donkey, drink like a camel and dance like a monkey on every single day off. My own private, full zoo.

Everything felt so real, so physical, so many various human reactions to negative emotions. All this was so disastrous that you would descent in it easily if you don't hit "the brakes". If you don't slow down you will "crash" badly. Right? Damn right!

Anyway, the mushroom business is quite slow in the summer, even slower with the heatwave. It was the hottest summer in the past eight years that year. Whoosh, the temperature of over twenty degrees lasted for weeks. Who remembered the last "heatwave" like this on the island?

In the summer, the mushroom business could only survive by producing so called "flats", the ones with big mushroom caps. The type of mushrooms which grow and need to be picked within 24 hours. None of the other mushrooms will appear on the surface of compost. Amen!

All of that massively affected mushroom pickers and their working patterns. Maybe two or three days a week of work! In other words, no job guaranteed!

Now, let me paint a picture for you of the relation between the mushroom business and pickers' behaviour. Within the seven days a week, we had at least three days off. What could we do in the middle of nowhere, far from the nearest shop, pub, civilisation? We had drinking parties! Oh, yeah, heavy drinking parties, so wild that "the locals" couldn't have imagined. The one party they would love to join, but they haven't been invited to. Why? Because of the language barrier on both sides.

Oh, yeah, party sounds brilliant! Another "wee", well... not so fast!

The reality checks here. You need to eat, pay the bills, you need money. To have a drinking party, you need money too. To have money, you need to work. Right? Vicious circle and constant choices: do you eat and pay the bills, or do you drink? Anyway, there was always someone with "a bottle" of alco.

"Oh, goodness me! Have mercy on my liver!!" I was really worried about my liver. I even gave up on my YOLO theme after a few days. I even pretended to be deaf and sick to get some rest from my mates. Nothing worked, there was virtually no place to hide from a drinking party.

So? Join it! Then, I was pretending to drink, then I was pretending that I was drunk and went to bed. I was pretending to be so drunk and dead to the world. Fake it until you make it. I have played my own game. The best part? My mates never knew about my drinking game. Damn, another Oscar nomination for me! Hah!

Apart from pretending at those drinking parties I had personal experiences with alco.

Let's start with Guinness. It's beautiful, tasty, refreshing, no commercial attached. I love it. Well, until I had eight pints of it and my kidneys stopped working. Total blockage, no single drop of urine for over twenty-four hours. Absolute shock to my urinary system and my whole body. My body was swollen, disfigured like the "Michelin" mascot. Again, no commercials, just painting a picture.

It took me another thirty-six hours to clear my body system and get back to my shape. *"OOPHH, that was rough. Just remember no more than four pints"* I had to make a mental note.

Moving to the "mushroom tent" as I used to call it, brought loads of mixed emotions caused by loads of various behaviours, cultures and personalities. It was like multi-cults orgy on a mental and physical level. Obviously, the master level of mixed languages too!

2.1 THE ENGLISH LANGUAGE

The spoken and mixed languages were: Polish, Russian, Lithuanian, Latvian, Ukrainian, and English. The last one, English was broken like "Me love, me no eat." It was perfectly understood and served well for work purposes. The choice of language didn't matter when we were talking about work, we all knew what we were talking about.

On the social level, the English language was below the basic level. The grammar of English did not exist. I will paint the picture for you here. I have met a nice "local" guy. By "local" I mean Irish[4]. I was getting used to the Irish accent, but my English was still "in its infancy", despite my little act at the airport worth the Oscar nomination.

I invited the local fellow into our "mushroom tent" for one of our parties. My roommate was always welcoming everyone, despite her massive language barrier. The top attribute of our culture is our hospitality. The rule number one is: the guest needs to be fed, whether he or she wants it or not! My roommate was on her hospitality mission. With her best efforts, she tried to

---

4 Yes! NO offence, but to avoid offending anyone on the Irish island due to history, politics, and religious beliefs I use the term "local, locals." For those who know the history of the island my reason is clear, I hope. For others, please check history books ☺.

ask my guest if he was hungry. Bear with me because I cannot transcribe the sound she was making, but that hilarious conversation went like this:

With her gestures showing shuffling something into her mouth, she made a Polish sound the equivalent of yummy in English. In other words, she was saying, "yummy, yummy, yummy" and 'shuffling' invisible food into her mouth, like you would be encouraging a baby to eat.

My guest was totally puzzled. My roommate was unstoppable in her efforts and convinced that she was doing everything to show her hospitality. I was rolling on the floor, laughing so hard that I almost peed myself. They both looked at me like I was crazy! Because they totally understood one another. My local friend said, "No, thanks! I want drink." My roommate was trying again and again for a few minutes. I had to stop her, but I was powerless as I was laughing. Finally, she gave up. That was a great laugh and every time I recall that scene, I have my "LMFAO" time like I have lost my senses!

Another "bump" to learning the English language was the Irish accent. Woo, it was a tough one at the beginning, but I had a chance to practice it almost every day with our friendly taxi driver. She was a super nice and hard-working lady. She put so much effort into understanding me, and vice versa. After a few weeks of travelling together, we were sharing jokes on the way to the mushroom farm. Sometimes we were sharing our worries. Of course, with both of our different accents confusion was inevitable, but we always managed to laugh in the end.

Our chats and my accent affected her way of speaking to her own children. One day, she brought her children home from school, and she was trying to explain to them what she was going to make for dinner. She was talking to them very slowly and almost paused between words like she was talking to me.

One of her children protested, "Mum, I am twelve! Why do you talk to me like I am four years old?" Next day she asked me,

""I didn't notice that I do that! Am I doing something wrong?"
"No, you aren't. You are so used to talking to me that you have
lost your own pace of speech." I was laughing, but I felt for her.
"Come on, try to speak to me like you did before we met." I encouraged her and it worked for me, too. I was getting into the speed.

Learning the English language is a skill like exercising mus-
cles, but understanding the Irish accent is the master level worth
the damn World Cup!

By the way, the average English speaker born and raised
in England does not understand an Irish-English speaker and
vice versa. Not to mention a Scottish accent that confuses and
sounds like harsh noises to the other two English speakers.
Anyway, I love them all!

2.2 THE RUSSIAN LANGUAGE

The common language at work and at "the mushroom tent" was
Russian and all real and fancy combinations of it. Most of us had
just basics of Russian. Some of us didn't even have that. But we
were learning on the go. For example, if a Lithuanian speaker
couldn't find the right word in Russian, then they used English.
If they couldn't find the right word in either language, then they
used a Lithuanian word. The others learnt Lithuanian.

Something like this: "Ačiū for gloves" [phonetic- Atchoo] in
Lithuanian means thank you.

Absolutely fantastic experience! Something new was always
hanging around. That new word in another language had one
powerful goal: we wanted to talk to each other. It didn't matter
what language we used. Even if there were not words to express
our thoughts, we used gestures and/or the whole-body language
to communicate. There are so many universal gestures and body
postures that you can use to tell a story without words. We were
unstoppable and creative in our communication. We had so much
fun! There were tears of laughter and tears for sadness sometimes. But we communicated anyway because we wanted to!

F.Y.I. – Misunderstandings between Eastern European nationalities have not only historical backgrounds, but also political, linguistic, and cultural context. Especially the animosities between Polish and Russians.

Though I am not going to explain it here. I have grown up in "deep" communism, and I had to learn the Russian language at school. But I always had my own view and opinions that helped me to understand the difference between "system" and "culture", intuitively. I just knew that instinctively, but only now I do understand why I was seeing things that way.

Despite overall disapproval of being forced to learn the Russian language, I actually like the language. Well, it is another language in my personal collection, my extra feature. I like different languages, it's my "thing". It is my blessing!

The only difference is how do you learn a language. Are you forced to do it or is it a need or is it a pleasure?

The first option is being forced at school. For any GCSE in the UK, you must choose at least one modern foreign language. Then you are forcing yourself to learn it in the name of passing the exam. Actually, you are memorising vocabulary, grammar, not so much of communicative skills. After the exam, all of it immediately evaporates from your mind. Well, maybe a single word or two hanging loosely between brain cells and occasionally showing up when something triggers the memory. Other than that, "you do not use it, you lose it".

The other two options of learning language were vividly explained to me by my Russian friend. In his humble opinion, there are two ways to learn how to communicate in any language. The first option is to spend a significant amount of time in a local jail for committed crime. It is a need to communicate with cell mates and others in order to survive. It is a really hard and not recommended way.

The second one is to get married to a native speaker of any language. Oh, this is a super pleasurable way to learn any language on top of anything else. Using this variant, my friend has learnt four different languages with four wives! And his wife

No. 5 is a Russian native speaker! All around the world to find the one who speaks the same language! It worked for him! The downside to this option is an expensive divorce. Though, you need to pay for your private language lessons!

That option also worked for me to some extent, until the expensive part appeared, the divorce.

Nevertheless, there are more variants for learning any language, but the most important ingredient is the love for a language. The dedication to learn, take it with ease not with pain, not with force but pleasure. Listen to music, watch movies in the language you love, even if someone questions your sanity when you talk to yourself out loud in a foreign language. Well, in that case, if you need to explain yourself, tell them that you are preparing for the role of your life. Or just ignore them! You love the language, full stop.

For a few weeks, the multi-language "mushroom tent" was packed to the rafters with different people. At some points, there were fourteen of us. There was an atmosphere of summer camp. There were friends and enemies, love, broken hearts, personal dramas, alliances and "lonely wolves". The energies of all of us and our emotions were so intense and charged that I am surprised it did not consume the whole village with a massive fire!

2.3 ADVENTUROUS TRANSPORTATION
ON THE GREEN ISLAND

Back then, I mean many full moons ago, the transportation in the Republic of Ireland was a surprising adventure every single time. On working days, we were going to work with our lovely lady taxi driver. However, usually we didn't know what time we would finish work, so our bosses or workmates with cars were taking us home. Would you guess how many passengers can fit into a VW Passat? Six? Seven? Nahhh… Eight passengers plus driver! Nine in total, all in the cabin, zero in the boot. What was more, it was 20km distance to drive, about a 40-minute journey. I know, there are places where people still travel in more extreme conditions, but that one was kind of personal to me on many levels.

Also, the public transport at the time, from our village to the nearest town (about 20km) went twice a day. One in the morning and one in the evening and never on time. The timetable existed in the parallel world. I never knew if I already missed the bus or it hadn't arrived yet. Usually I missed it anyway, so I walked that half marathon distance, or I've tried to stop any car that was going in the same direction. *"Not a big deal, I have tried hitch-hiking before on the continent,"* I thought. Then I had my few attempts that proved me wrong. My personal AHA moments!

The gist was in the location, the continent vs the island!

Just the example of hitch-hiking on the continent, there is 798km between the Polish border with Germany (A) and Amsterdam (B). I travelled that distance with two friends in twelve hours from A to B, including swapping three cars on the way. Waiting for the one driver who would stop to take three strangers on board. Only three cars and only twelve hours!

Now, on the green island, on average, it was taking four hours and three cars to travel 20km! *"What the hell?"* I thought that it was some conspiracy against all hitch-hikers here. Well, I was close. So, I asked one of my lift drivers "Why is that?" The driver explained it clearly. "If someone tries to stop any car on the road, it means:

A) You are not local. Locals have cars. If they don't have cars, they have family to give them a lift.
B) You are not local; you are dangerous – locals' mind-set.
C) A Single woman on the road? – It was a big 'NO, NO' in certain, traditional understanding, etc. Loosely translated: you are not a lady if you are alone on the road.

In other words, you are not one of us. "I would rather avoid you than take any risks," the driver summarised. Well, fair enough! Thankfully for me, there were enough "nosy" locals to give me a lift, anyway.

I used "nosy" on purpose. One Irish lady explained to me the Irish meaning of the word. "We are not nosy, we are curious." Again, fair enough, worked for me.

There were two more things that made the whole journey more "exciting and adrenaline pumping". The country roads and drivers' skills. According to some people Irish country roads were built following marks made by "cows pissing while they were walking". The widths of roads that could fit two bicycles but not two cars were definitely challenging for all drivers. Especially for lorry drivers! I had the privilege of watching their skills from the cabin of one of the lorries. It was like in those reality shows of the "Extreme Drivers". Two lorries were passing one another, with a space of one inch between their side mirrors. I watched their manoeuvres with "jaw dropped" and the excitement of a five year old watching the magical performance. "*WOOOOW, how do they do it?*" No clue, but they have my absolute and sincere salute for their skills!

As the whole experience of travelling across the green island grew on me systematically, my only thought was "*get used to it.*" With limited choices, I went with alignment and flow to keep the sense of adventure rather than punishment and dark side of transformation.

My personal level of transformation was going through rough, black paths. Limited financial sources and the close circle of people from the same industry. They felt helpless, as did I. In other words, without connections outside "the circle" the chances for any improvement did not exist. At least it appeared so. In the past, the internet was publicly accessible at libraries or very, very "wealthy" households. There were private businesses that allowed anyone to use the internet per hour but in cities, maybe towns. Not in villages! Definitely not in the village where I was living at the time. Mainly for that reason I was taking those trips to the nearest town, to get access to the internet and the world!

Well, limits, barriers and restrictions were the only things I could've seen then.

My "inner being" was screaming *"are you fricking joking me? Is this all? Picking mushrooms, drinking parties, travelling like a tramp for the rest of my life? This is not for me. I have a different pathway, different 'calling', places to be! Hey, listen to me! Move on, follow your call, you can do it. I know you can because I can, so you can too. Believe me, trust me and follow me, your intuition, your authentic you, your inner being. Hello? Yes, you, move your logical, realistic, physical being RIGHT NOW!"*

My own response to my "inner being" was like: *"AHA, sure and would you be so kind and tell me how am I supposed to do it?"* Back then I was sarcastic and critical to the whole world around me. That also included myself. Darkness all around, tunnelled vision and nothing but obstacles. No light at the end of the tunnel! By the way, do not go towards the light in the tunnel. It is a train!

On second thought: *"What if I can do it? If I can change it? If I do and get something different, better? What if I try here and now? What do I have to lose?"* The whole "what if..." started calling me in my "daydreaming". Visualisations were coming from nowhere, just thoughts, pictures, feelings full of shivers and thrills. Waves of uplifting emotions to see those pictures of happiness, fun, love, freedom in the rhythm of music. There is the one tune that was able to shift my positive energy and mood from "zero to millions of energy sparks" within fifteen seconds. The tune is house, trans type of music, not my "cup of tea" at all in terms of music but for some reason it works for me, every time, even now. So let it do its best! I play it over and over on my speakers, headphones and in my head.

"Let it be," I thought. So after ten weeks that went by in a blink of an eye, I have made a very bold decision to move out from *"the mushroom tent".* Even though my tourist visa expired after being extended a second time for another four weeks and my legal residence period passed already. Also, I left behind some connections with certain people and the burden of their energies. I had to stand up for myself to protect my needs, my future. My bold, assertive step was shocking to some.

I was looking for my own path, my reasons, my future, I was just searching for MYSELF. Although it was more like looking for the black cat in the pitch-black room. There was no chance to find it. *"Damn, I need bloody light,"* I thought.

Someone said: "instead of waiting for the light at the end of the tunnel, go down and light it up yourself." *"Phi, fair enough, I am on my way. But which direction should I chose? To the left, of course."* Against all odds, I "dived" into an unknown territory completely out of my comfort zone. That was my left. How deep should I go? To the damn "bottom of the Hell itself!"

. . . .

Acceptance is a KEY! Yes, it is! Between no option and just one option, an acceptance plus gratitude equals ease with any adjustments and necessary changes. It's a temporary solution that gives you the opportunity to be vulnerable and adjust to contrasts. It's like a survival camp to build your emotional resilience. Time and patience will lead you to see clearly what works for you and what doesn't.

Remove toxicity from your life ASAP

Let go of toxic emotions, people, and places. Release it all with love and thankfulness. After all, they gave you great lessons, served their purpose to shift your emotional expansion. Now! Let it go!

In the meantime, breathe! Breathing helps to relieve your stress, gives distance to the current situation, slows down your heart rate, brings clarity and restores focus.

Combine breathing with mindfulness, and you will fly fearlessly between life's contrast. Check details in Your Daily Exercises part.

Be curious or nosy (your choice!), discover new languages, new cultures. All for new adventurous testing of "open waters", testing your boundaries, your skills, or learning new skills and expanding your personal experiences.

YOUR DAILY EXERCISES

Self-Acceptance

a. Embrace yourself exactly as you are; with all your thoughts, emotions, feelings, perceptions and skills. You are UNIQUE.
b. Allow yourself to be who you are with all your strengths and weaknesses. Make a list of your strengths and achievements. What are your talents, your abilities and traits that make – YOU who you are.
c. Check your weaknesses; you might find some areas for improvement whenever possible. However, do not hold to them as "must do" things, rather concentrate on your strengths. Imperfections are perfect lessons for future achievements.
d. Quality social connections are important for happiness. Bond with those who are like-minded.
e. Forgive yourself the mistakes made in the past. Give yourself permission to learn from those valuable lessons. Take what is important for your next step and move on. You cannot change the past, but you still can create a better future.
f. There are many things you cannot control, accept them, and focus on things you can control (e.g., your emotions, your progress, your expansion).

Those are only a few key points of acceptance, but you can check for more on Happiness.com[5].

Breathing techniques

In complex situations when you are anxious, stressed, under pressure, use the breathing technique described below. Your body gives you signals when those extreme feelings are taking

---

5 12 ways to practise self-acceptance | happiness.com

over; your heartbeat increases, you are sweating, it is difficult to breathe, blood pressure pumps in your temples, blurred vision.

Start by breathing out first. Force a strong breath out. Deep breath in and breathe out. Then deep breath in through your nose. Breathe out through your mouth. Repeat six times and breathe normally. You can do it whenever and wherever you feel that you have lost your emotional balance. That simple exercise will help you to regain control over your feelings, it will bring calmness and clarity to your mind.[6]

Practice Mindfulness

Mindfulness means "to be and feel here and now". It helps to calm your brain and your emotions.

It serves to keep your mind completely focused on the one easy task.

Mindfulness allows your mind to shift focus in a non-judgmental way. You don't label your initial thoughts, emotions, or sensations as good or bad.

Mindfulness is easy to learn and practice. It's as easy as brushing teeth! It is recommended to brush your teeth for a minimum of 2 minutes. That's the time you can practice mindfulness, too.

You will give your brain 2 minutes' recovery time from multi-tasking. You will give yourself mental relief while keeping your mouth healthy. Your dentist will be proud of your great brushing skill; you will save money on dental treatment.

Most importantly, you will take care of your mental health.

Try it!

---

6 https://youtu.be/YCc8OD19eMA

Brushing your teeth, ideally twice a day, gives you the opportunity to practice mindfulness twice a day!

You will reach Master level in less than a month.

While you are brushing your teeth, bring your entire focus to the task. Notice everything that is going on in your mouth.

Smell the toothpaste, place it on your toothbrush, slowly. Put the toothbrush into your mouth, taste it.

Consciously choose upper or lower jaw first, then proceed to a side of your mouth and continue there.

Feel the brush touching your teeth, one by one. Then feel it touching your gums and the sides of your tongue.

Watch it in the mirror, count manoeuvres, listen to the sound of the brush movements. Slowly move brush from one side of your mouth to the other.

Stay focused on your task and repeat the same on the other jaw. Feel it, taste it, listen to the brush movements.

Check water for rinsing your teeth. Is it cold, warm? Hold the water in your mouth.

How does it feel in your mouth? Rinse your teeth slowly, hold the water in your mouth, then spit it out.

Touch your teeth with your tongue from side to side. Do they feel clean?

Do you need flossing? If so, go through every single space between your teeth with an entire focus in each space and movement.

Make a mental checklist for brushing teeth, to see if you've done everything well.

Congratulations! You just completed your first mindfulness practice! Your brain and your teeth are extremely grateful for those 2 minutes!

2.4 THE HELL JUST OPENED

I moved to the shared accommodation in the small town. The difference between the village and the small town was in the number of streets and pubs. The small town had four streets and two more pubs than the village. The pubs were more entertaining, live music, pool, and dance floors in some. Our parties shifted to the next level.

One of the strong arguments for me to move to the small town was the walking distance to work. It was about 40 minutes' walk or 10 minutes' drive, both options acceptable for me. I shared our new spacious and comfortable flat with 3 more people. All of us worked in the same mushroom business, just different teams. Our mix of nationalities and languages expanded by the Czech language. From my perspective, Czech language and the way it is expressed, sounds like a polish four year old telling a funny story. I will tell some stories about it later.

One more big pro for the flat was the pub underneath, just under our stairs. *"Superb, I can go downstairs in my sleepers,"* I laughed, but not for long.

The mushroom season began, and the business was getting busier every day. The farm was growing and expanding. It was good for the owners and, to some extent, for us pickers. The pickers worked for at least 14 hours a day. Yeah! Just to clarify, we were paid per crate of mushrooms, not per hour! There were only three local ladies paid per hour and worked from 8am till 4pm, maybe 5pm. The rest of the pickers, I mean the whole Eastern European team, worked from 5-6am until the whole "flash" was done. Most of a time we finished around 8-9pm. Day by day, Monday till Sunday, every day. We had a day off in a fortnight, if so. Or called sick without being paid. Other than that, no excuses. Though, there were some days we finished just before midnight! On such occasions we faced a dilemma, should we take time to travel to and from work not getting enough sleep. Going home and coming back five hours later didn't make much sense. Well, no work, no money, simple. Complain about working conditions, our rights?

To whom? Not really, because most of us were illegal. AHA! Yes, it was a full version of modern slavery, non-trafficking, forced labour. Non-trafficking because we went there by ourselves! Our bosses knew that and used that with the full intention of exploiting every single one of us for their own profits.

We tried to persuade them to ease the tension and it worked for a little while. However, their business was expanding, and they invested more in the farm. With this expansion they needed help/assistance of a production manager. They hired The Man, The Squirrel.

One glance at The Man, I knew trouble had just arrived. The Man got a nickname corresponding with his appearance, I called him – the Squirrel. Squirrels in Poland are ginger! Dah! The Squirrel was coldly polite towards us and always managed a professional distance. When I was standing a few feet away from him, I could feel the Polar air radiating from him. Brrrr... still gives me chills. A completely ambivalent and emotionless individual with a key focus on increasing production. The simple formula of any business, more production equals more profit. More cheap production equals even more profit. Well, we didn't have much choice like only to accept the presence of the Squirrel. At least in the beginning.

In the meantime, we tried to be brave, work hard, complain less, and laugh more. Only females were mushroom pickers. Delivering and removing compost was hard work and it was done by men.

Also, it was men who collected crates and loaded lorries. So, no men were in a mushroom house when pickers were there.

So, only women were sharing their fantasies, dreams and reality in mushroom houses. No matter the age difference or civil status within pickers, there was one topic we shared, like housewives.

"Let's talk about sex baby...," Do you know this tune? I wonder, it was in the 90s, I think.

That "topic" could just pop out, completely out of a non-related conversation. Only because one of us had a random association with a single word in a conversation. Boom, the "topic" was on and for that, some days were hilarious. Even local ladies were laughing a lot with us. Of course, only if I precisely translated the joke into English.

Picking mushrooms is a manual task we performed using trolleys with all the required equipment. You have to pay attention to a mushroom's size to pick, scale it and place in correct punnets according to size and weight. In other words, hands and eyes of pickers were busy, but not minds. Our minds were doing "free-falling" in producing frivolous thoughts, images then words to keep ours spirits up. Of course, universal gestures and body language were used regularly to fill in gaps of missing words in any language used. Sometimes, scales, buckets with rubbish, punnets and other equipment were thrown out of the trolleys and flying in the air due to our vigorous chats about sex.

Why flying in the air? Well, the construction of four levels of shelves with mushroom beds was over four meters high. Upper levels, three and four had hanging trolleys, and required two pickers to set them on the right level. The trolley itself was heavy, with equipment it could weigh almost one hundred kilograms. The picker was manually pulling whole that weight!

Moreover, getting on and off the trolley on the fourth level was a gymnastic effort. Climbing over the second and third levels of shelves to get to the top level was a part of the daily task. Once we were at the top it was just a matter of pulling the shelves alongside. Dropping something from the trolley while hanging on the upper levels was the worst nightmare. Usually someone from the team could help pick the fallen item, and with few attempts throw it up to the top level. Only throwing knives was forbidden! Although, many times, pickers had to go up and down multiple times to sort things out.

The circulation on the two top levels was horrendous. Pickers were working on both sides of shelves at the same time. A picker on the third level would be approaching from the left end of the shelf and a picker on the fourth level from the right. They would meet at some point of the shelf. Both pickers had to remove all the equipment from their trolleys to swap them and to continue working along the level. Usually, at that point our conversations were going like this:

"Watch out, I am coming at your head!" said the picker from the top level.

"Wow, good that it's my head you are aiming at, not the other place. I don't want to get pregnant," responded the picker from the lower level, and the whole team was in stitches.

That one comment made our day, and the sex theme went on and on all day long. Multiple objects including knifes were flying around as we laughed hard on two top levels of mushrooms shelves. Thankfully, no one got hurt, but the risk of an injury was constantly present. Those acrobatic figures a picker had to do to get to the higher levels or risk of falling from those levels could cause serious injuries.

Well, I was usually working on the top level. I liked to be there on the top. It gave me a view on everything that was going on in the mushroom house. It gave me time to visualise my future, my pathway. It gave me a chance to sing badly and loudly, and no one could stop me. I knew the risk and took it with a faith that everything is always working out for me. I never fell off the trolley, and I never injured myself or anyone from the team. Yeah, the top was good for me then!

Apart from moving and swapping trolleys, the size of mushrooms was often another reason for a sex theme to our chat and for laughter. Usually there were three sizes of mushroom to pick up, determined by the radius of its cap in millimetres. You may wonder what it has to do with sex? The size matters! Well, picture that!

One picker said: "If that is the right size of the mushroom cap, I can say that I have never seen five hundred millimetres in my life. It's too small!"

"Have you seen bigger?" said the other picker.

"You need glasses!" someone else shouted.

"I have seen bigger..." the first responded with a cheeky smile and tone of voice. The creativity of the team was automatically going up in terms of the sex topic. We were on a standby to jump into the conversation.

"Without glasses?" added another picker.

"Was it mushroom?" absolutely naively asked the other picker. The team was suffocating, laughing their heads off.

"Nah, it was a penis!" the first picker replied and continued: "Although, I am not sure how to explain it. Anyone knows what European size is?" The first picker went on. That was it! We were laughing and shared theories, experiences about men's genitalia, like size matters, technique matters. One human organ and almost endless divagation about it with bursts of laughter and funny disagreements. Still, none of us could answer the first picker's question.

One of our yardmen entered the mushroom house in the middle of our hilarious chat. He was young and new on the farm, and also completely unaware of our conversations.

"I need to take five hundreds. Lorry is waiting," he said.

The first picker just glanced at him, didn't even stop picking mushrooms and said without hesitation, "You must have European size!" The whole team burst out and roared with laughter. The poor guy froze, went pale, turned on the heel and ran out of the house. We were in stitches for good ten minutes! Another man came, he knew us well. One look at us and he knew what was going on.

"You witches! You scared the crap out of him!" he yelled with a big grin on his face. "What have you told him?" he was curious. We couldn't speak, constantly laughing, so he had to wait a bit for an explanation. Once we told him, he joined us in our laughter, but he didn't answer the question. He left us wondering even more about the European size.

It was one of those long days, working so many hours that we needed something trivial and simple to laugh about. We needed distraction from our reality, and we desperately needed time off.

• •

By doing or saying something childish, silly, or totally inappropriate you are increasing your positive vibrations. LAUGH! LAUGH! AND LAUGH more. It really helps.

YOUR DAILY EXERCISES

Laugh

Don't laugh every day, laugh every minute. Laugh with others. Laugh on your own. Find a comedy movie, stand-up, funny videos, read funny book. Laugh out loud and expand your lungs, get more oxygen into your body and produce positive chemicals in your brain. Laughing relieves pain, stress, relaxes your body, boosts the immune system and makes you happier.

2.5 DAYS OFF NOT FOR RELAX

Every now and then we would get a day off, but not too often during the mushroom season. Oh, how splendid! Unfortunately our options were limited. What should I do? Go shopping in the bigger town maybe? We needed a car with a driver. Nah, not available. Cook something nice? Who wants to stay in the kitchen on the day off? Nah, not ideal. Visit the local library and use the internet? Oh yes, only it was Sunday. Damn. Home SPA? Well, not such a bad idea, let's try that. Picking clothes at the local charity shop? Oh, yes, that was fun too, but again it was Sunday! Damn! It was unbelievably limited! But we tried our best.

A kind of "home SPA" done, washing done, house cleaned. What's next? We needed more FUN! And so we had fun assisted by tequila shots, we drifted between three pubs with pool tables. With every shot of tequila, our games got better, at least mine did. The locals were watching us with adoration and curiosity. *"How the heck can they drink that much and play so well"* I could see that in their faces. The answer was: Not a clue! I surprised myself too – not only with games, but also with me drinking tequila. To my surprise, me and tequila have a mutual "understanding". Well, I knew exactly when the next shot may have "dramatic" effects on my body. But my mate The Hen, she did not know her limits with tequila.

At the end of our party, I had to tow The Hen on my back to our flat. She was barely moving her legs, mumbling something about more games.

"Not today, sweetheart, not today." I was calming her down and helping her into bed. I put myself into my bed, and I went out like the electricity during blackout.

The next morning, we were up for work at 5 in a morning accompanied by "a killer" hangover. I came into the kitchen where The Hen was already making coffee. She was crying that she could barely stand on her legs and her head was "banging". I was a bit better, but not much. "Just shoot me. I want to go back to bed," I cried.

In my head, the song *"never again"* was playing over and over. *"I don't drink like that. What is wrong with me?"* Well, I didn't know then, but it was my coping mechanism for all my suffering, lost dreams, lost hope. *"It was not what I was hoping for! Well, I knew it would take time to make things work. But how much longer? How can I make another move? And where can I go?"* My thoughts were unclear and fearful because I knew I was there illegally. *"You are not going anywhere, not soon anyway; you have no papers. Make peace with that."* Those thoughts were devastating!

We survived that day on the farm, but it turned out that we were not the only ones with hangovers. Most pickers came to work with hangovers or still drunk! Oh, yes! Almost all of us had similar dilemmas and reasons to drink, a kind of "pickers-alcoholics social club".

Alcohol was not our exclusive entertainment. The other one regarded "the love stories". Those stories were mainly accompanied by alcohol. Not many cared that for some people those emotions were real and heart-breaking. The audience was waiting for juicy "love stories" brought by gossiping individuals. I have always found all that gossiping to be hideous, possibly because I was a victim of those "big mouthing" creatures a few times. Although, anywhere in the world, on a daily basis people are still craving for a drama. Society often believes men and women cannot just be friends, there must be sex involved. *"Give me a break! I always had three, four men friends and only two, three girlfriends."* I thought. Me and the social models, we exist in parallel worlds, the social model has nothing to do with me.

Living with so many different people of mixed cultures and genders helped me to understand those relationships better. In our shared flat, my closest man friend was The Hawk, a Czech. We had a similar sense of humour, and we also shared the passion for learning the English language. He taught me how to drive a car with the steering wheel on the right side and he trusted me with driving his car later. Most importantly, like me, The Hawk wanted to move away to the bigger town and to get a better job. We were close; we were honest with each other.

We supported one another, and we shared our dreams. As good friends do, we shared everything except sex. We were more like siblings. Although, people we were working with have seen it differently and they were creating our "love story", talking behind our backs.

Intuitively, I trusted The Hawk's honesty, and I knew he has no feelings or intentions toward me other than friendship. Once, The Hen came to me with a grand speech about The Hawk's feelings.

"You are blind, You witch! The Hawk loves you and you are hurting him so much when you are going out with this DJ. He goes 'bananas' when DJ calls you on his mobile. The Hawk is crazy in love with you!" The Hen was raging.

"What are you talking about?" I was confused. *"Did I make a mistake in terms of our friendship?"* I thought. I knew that I didn't love him, and I was convinced that he felt the same way. *"I need to talk to him, now! Well, after work."* I was already making a plan in my head. The Hawk was working late that day, so I had a chance to get us beer after work and wait for him at home.

"Hi, what is the occasion?" he asked in Czech when he walked into the kitchen.

"We need to talk," I said seriously in Polish.

"Ooooh, I am scared when a woman says, 'We need to talk.'" He laughed.

"Yeah, you should be," I said with a serious face.

"OK, now you are really scaring me." He changed his tone of voice. "What's going on?" he asked.

"Sit down, have a beer and let's be honest here," I instructed him, then I explained the issue. Through my whole speech he looked at me with an absolutely straight face, fully focused on what I was saying.

"Please tell me that I wasn't wrong?" I almost begged him. The Hawk was sitting still, sipping beer with the facial expression of a mackerel impressed in the stone. No muscle moved. Then he burst into hysterical laughter. He had a really great, contagious laugh. The Hawk made the whole impression of the Laughing My Ass Off on the kitchen floor. Honestly, for the first three seconds of this show I froze, then the "AHA" moment came, and I joined him on the floor, laughing hard. The noise we made brought our other two flatmates into the kitchen. The Hen and Sloth stood at the door and looked at us, rolling and laughing on the floor like two weirdos. They were completely confused and ready to call a doctor thinking we lost our minds.

The Hawk caught his breath and whispered, "No, you weren't wrong." And he laughed even harder. Tears were rolling down my face from laughing so hard. Then, although my vision was blurred I caught the facial expressions of both the Hen and Sloth, and I've lost it even more.

"You two were wrong," I screamed at them. Without a single word, those two turned around and walked away to their rooms. I swear, I could see their "tails" between their legs as they were walking. Clearly, they were disappointed. No more drama here.

Me and The Hawk spent some time on the floor calming down and talking more about our friendship. For the sake of fun, we made a pact to keep others on the mushroom farm in the dark and continue our "love show". The next few days we were acting like "lovers", sending kisses in the air and we called each other sweet nicknames. We were so convincing as 'a couple' that most of our co-workers believed in us. We had fun, and we didn't care about those gossips. Apart from us only our flatmates knew the truth, but they didn't bother to correct others. What is more, they actually joined us in our performance. They finally got the idea of FUN!

The friendship between me and The Hawk got stronger after that. We had each other's backs at all times.

The Hawk's close friend and his "shadow" was "Sloth", also Czech. Yes, "Sloth" was his nickname and it fully described his personality. Sloth was slow, or rather phlegmatic in moving and thinking, but not retarded. Our Sloth was exactly like that. He was nice and gentle with a specific sense of humour, compatible with the rest of us, but extremely slow in everything. Sometimes The Hawk and Sloth had discussions in Czech about something serious. The Hawk tried to explain something, he was a passionate speaker. Sloth was completely opposite, and it took him a very long time to respond to The Hawk's comments; this irritated The Hawk extremely. Honestly, they were a living example of opposites attraction. Watching them two while having a heated discussion was my best entertainment. Every time they had an argument, I had the best fun ever. While I was watching them, I laughed so hard that I had muscle spasms in my face and tummy. The Czech language sounds to me like a parody of any other language. I still can't keep a straight face when I listen to it.

Of course, The Hawk didn't find it funny; me laughing when he was seriously cross with something or someone, then he would say to me:

"*Oy 'pszonka' [pshoncka] stop laughing!*" He yelled at me. 'Pszonka' is a nickname Check speakers use for Polish people. In Polish, we use loads of consonants like "sz-sh", "cz-ch", to Czechs and others, it sounds like moving sand paper against a wooden board – shoo, shoo, shoo. Those consonants are difficult from the phonetic point of view, and it takes loads of time to learn how to pronounce them.

Over the time we have spent together, our friendship was tested a few times. Our trio, me, The Hawk and Sloth had a mutual understanding and we wouldn't take everything personally so we could afford to laugh at each other without hurting anyone.

Having that kind of friendship during tough times was a blessing. They both gave me safety and support that allowed me to focus on myself and the future. Most of all, I needed romance and fun.

. . . .

Be grateful for your friends, especially for those who make you laugh. They are your blessings. Be kind to them. You need to LAUGH greatly: on your own and in a good company! You also need LOVE, but love yourself first to understand how you want to be loved!

Just love them and be grateful for their presence in Your life!

Also, let them go when they need to go – no hard feelings.

YOUR DAILY EXERCISES

Count your blessings

Appreciate Yourself and every aspect of Your life. Giving thanks for small things will help you realise the good things in your life and will allow you to focus on them rather than dwelling on negative ones.

2.6 MY WEE ROMANCES

I was aiming more at fun and adventure than romance. As I was experimenting with different cultures and testing shallow waters of diversity, I was also learning a lot about myself. Although, I didn't know how far away I was from myself then.

Well, being away from home for a few months I was still thinking about my ex. *"I wonder if you still think about me. Was our relationship real? Well, to me it was real. What went wrong?".* Memories and reflections were running through my mind sometimes. I was looking for some answers. I tried to understand my feelings, emotions, and reasoning behind my actions. Oh, it was so hard! Being abroad on my own, illegally, working like a slave without "The One" to love and to be loved. Can you see what I didn't know then? Can you see how far I was from myself? I needed someone to love me, but I didn't love myself. I was "The One" who should love myself, but I didn't know that.

I tried to contact my "ex" a few times, but he said he was too busy even for a short chat. Once I called, he told me to hold because he was in the middle of something. "But I don't have enough credit to wait." I tried to explain, but he didn't listen. I hung up. *"I am not going to call you again!"* I thought to myself. It was bitter knowing that someone I had spent years with and dedicated my feelings and time to, had no time to talk. *"Oh, F&^&^ You!"* That day my bubble was burst! I realised that it was over. There was nothing else to talk about and nothing was holding me there. I started burying my feelings, alcohol and parties were my form of grieving. We all grieve differently!

"I am a free woman, and I can have fun being single! OK, Let's get some romance." I tried to cheer myself up.

With a bunch of pickers, we went to the local pub. DJ was playing good party music. Of course, we had a few shots too many, and dancing was going a bit crazy. DJ picked up our wild party mood precisely and played even better music to keep the party going. Back then, the last round of drinks was announced just before 1am, then at 1am the national anthem was played.

It was like, "Well, folks, finish your drinks and get out of here."
After 1am, we still had drinks, and DJ came to me asking for
my number. "Damn! My phone is broken, but if you want, I can
give you my mate's number so you can contact me." I was hoping that The Hawk would not kill me for giving his number. *"I
will explain it to The Hawk later,"* I thought on the spot. The Hawk
knew that my phone was broken, anyway.

"OK, we can do that," DJ said, and we exchanged numbers.
"One more thing. Are you single?" DJ asked.

"Yes, I am, no worries," I said with confidence. Then I realised it was a huge relief to say that.

"Can I call you tomorrow?" DJ asked.

"Of course you can," I assured him. Wow, that was some speed
towards fun!

When we were leaving the pub, all the pickers were cheering us
on to have a kiss. We kissed and said "Good night" like separated
lovers. The whole pack went on even louder cheering, for the fun
they were having and the free entertainment DJ and I provided.

"The hell with you all. It's my time to have fun and romance!"
I shouted to them, laughing. I was happy again!

Before I had a chance to explain anything to The Hawk about
this, DJ sent a text message with kisses and saying good night,
again. The Hawk knocked on my door, then walked in with his
phone in hand and sticking it in my face.

"Is this for you?" he asked.

"Oh, yes. I am sorry I didn't tell you about it sooner." I was
happy, and I had to improvise on the spot. "I am sorry! Please
help me here. You know my phone is broken. It will take me a
few more weeks to sort it out." I was begging.

"Alright, but I hope he is not going to call in the middle of
the night," The Hawk said softly.

"I will tell him, no worries." I promised and sent a text to
DJ. I asked what time he was going to call me the next day and
I told him not to call at night. DJ quickly replied that he will
text first around 4pm, then call.

The next afternoon, The Hawk knocked on my door, again with his phone in his hand.

"Here, it's for you," he said calmly, but I could see that he was excited. Well, it was a new kind of entertainment in our small world filled with mushrooms.

DJ called to ask me out for a coffee. He picked me up an hour later. We went to the nearest lake for a chat, and later for a coffee. DJ was handsome, sensitive, gentle, and interesting. Magically he understood my basic English, and we had a pleasant conversation so we could get to know each other better.

I was happy. It felt sweet and innocent. My sweet new romance. It felt great being attracted to another human being, and fancied by a man who enjoyed my company and made me feel like a woman again. Oh, it was so good! I wanted that to last forever! Who wouldn't? Do you remember those first kisses, hugs, closeness that gave you goose bumps all over your body? Those butterflies in your stomach? Those chills running up and down your spine? Those rapid heartbeats every time your memory recalled all those sweet moments? Oh, yes, I bet you do, and I know that you wanted all of that to last forever. Right? Those first symptoms of joy, fulfilment, happiness, and love.

"Is this love?" I asked myself. Deep down, I was still hurt, and I didn't give myself enough time to heal. I jumped into the first available romance with the full force of hope that this time, this one exactly, this is real love. *"Aha? Are you for real woman?"* It was my next question. *"Wait and see what might happen. It might work, it might not, just give yourself time."* I tried to reason with myself but the idea of a simple romance and joy, of those sweet moments, never existed in my vocabulary. I simply never experienced that before as I was always attracted to rough individuals rather than romantic ones.

DJ was taking his time. He was kind and romantic, but to me it was like he couldn't decide what he wanted from me. Or simply, he couldn't communicate with me on the level I would understand. I couldn't blame him. At the same time, I was not able tell him many things I would express in normal circumstances but I was limited by the language barrier. A vicious circle! I guess we both suffered from frustration due to lack of communication, and three weeks later our sweet romance was over. DJ just informed me he is going to work more in the North. He can't see me often and he doesn't believe in a long distance relationship. *"Yeah, no distance relationship will last. I could tell you that. I am just putting the pieces of my heart together after that kind of relationship."* I tried to understand, but it was painful, again.

I made a decision the day DJ left. *"No man deserves my love and any attention except fun and play. But I deserve love and I love myself!"* I worked hard to get back on my YOLO theme that actually made few other people happy. Well, for example, The Hawk was happy about it. He didn't have to give up his phone for a few minutes a day, so I could send a text or receive a call from DJ.

• •

Love is within you. It is trust, compassion, and acceptance. You are pure love. "Loving yourself is not vanity, it is sanity." – Andre Gide.

The Power of positive self-talk makes its magical way to self-love. It's less than ONE minute! Check it in Your Daily Exercises.

YOUR DAILY EXERCISES

The Power of positive self-talk

The list of adjectives that you can add to the statement "I am…" is long, almost endless. Here are some starters: "I am enough." "I am worthy." "I am me." "I am unique." "I am healthy." "I am wealthy." "I am successful." "I am creative." "I am smart." "I am safe." "I am loved."

You can write down those prompts, but do not print them. The power is in your handwriting. Stick them all over your home, car, desk, computer, bathroom, carry them in your pocket. You can set a reminder on your phone! Honestly, the number of ideas is unlimited. Be bold and be creative with your personal affirmations.[7]

---

7 https://youtu.be/YCc8OD19eMA

2.7 PARTY TIME! LOVE, FALSE ALARM
AND SELF-DESTRUCTION

How to get back on the free-fall mojo? PARTY! Work hard and party even harder! With whom? Anybody who could keep up with my pace, drinks, and wild adventures, mainly co-workers.

It turned out that I wasn't the only one with a broken heart. One of my girlfriends was deeply in love with one of the boys who worked on the farm. Of course, the boy had his best friend; they were inseparable, like Siamese twins. That duo, kindly named by us "Dogs", worked together, travelled together, they were lived and partied together. They were so compatible on so many levels that one would be lost without the other one.

My girlfriend got a well-deserved nickname, "Witch". She was making all love spells and "poses" to get the attention of one of the Dogs, let's call him Doggy 1. One day she was this kind, sweet girl, sending love signals to Doggy 1. Another day, she pretended she was not interested in him at all. Doggy 1 knew about her amorous efforts. He made every effort to play hard to get or make her jealous. Of course, Doggy 2 was playing a full part in their game. I was watching them from a distance. It was clear to me that the Dogs' horseplay served to get her attention. The Witch needed a companion to go out, to chase Doggy 1, just to be close to him or to get on his nerves. I was the most suitable companion for her, whether for drinking and dancing or not drinking and driving us around nearby villages, all that to check on Doggy 1.

One party after another, the Witch and Doggy 1 were getting along, but not so close. Doggy 2 and I were watching them, but we got bored at some point, and spontaneously we had fun of our own. In the beginning, it was our intention just to show them how to have fun, just to encourage them. We made a whole damn show of provocative dances like lovers do, kisses, dance figures and touches. Nothing, Nada, null, they didn't get it. But we did, and a few parties later we moved on.

We had purely physical sex, no strings attached. Simple, physical pleasure of two adults. As we were busy encouraging another couple, we got so turned on that we couldn't stop ourselves from taking it to the next level. The performance unfolded into a spectacular display of genuine passion and intimacy, filled by an enchanting blend of kindness and effortless movements. It culminated in an exquisite and deeply satisfying simultaneous climax, capturing the true essence of our intimate connection. Huh, not a big deal! Oh, yes, it was a big deal. Not once, but many times and every time. We were surprised, astonished and speechless for a long time afterwards. We simply didn't expect that! It was just a show, and it was not supposed to end that way! Were we both so horny? Evidently, we were!

"Hello, woman, just a reminder, fun and only fun, nothing else." I was talking to myself loudly. I could do it even in his presence because Doggy 2 didn't speak Polish, just a few simple words in English and Russian.

Now, does it sound familiar? Just a few paragraphs ago, I was talking about the language barrier between lovers, right? Magically, I managed to get another one I couldn't communicate with in any language I knew. *"Damn! Lord! Have mercy! Please!"* I cried inside my head.

That night both Doggies and the Witch left my flat in silence. The only difference was that Doggy 2 was light and happy. The other, Doggy 1, was disappointed and rather frustrated and the Witch was in despair and angry. The next day on the farm, it was even more awkward. The Witch didn't talk to me at all. The Doggies behaved like a pair of clowns, completely ignoring the Witch and me. *"Oh well, let it be. Just this time - it doesn't matter,"* I thought to myself. Honestly, I couldn't be arse.

The Witch, though, couldn't let go of Doggy 1 and after a day of silent treatment for me, she came and asked for a favour.

"Oy, are you free tonight? I need a lift to a friend's house. I was wondering if you could get a car from The Hawk and help me, please!" she asked directly.

"I am free tonight. Only you need to ask The Hawk if he doesn't have plans. Then I can get his car for you," I replied. I didn't know her friend. I also didn't know that this friend she referred to was living in the same village as the Doggies. Again, I didn't care much, and I could do it easily, just for fun. The Witch went to The Hawk and asked to borrow his car. She promised him a full tank of petrol in return, which I was supposed to fill on the way back, but she was in a hurry and she forgot to tell me. When we were leaving the farm later, the Doggies were still working.

I picked the Witch up at her house and asked for directions.

"You know the village; it is not far from here," she said as I realised.

"Wait a minute, is it the village where the Doggies live?" I was really surprised.

"Uhm, yes, the very same," she said, as if it was nothing.

"Oy, just tell me, what are you planning to do over there?" I got curious. I was a part of her plan, so I deserved to know that.

"Oh, nothing, I really need to talk to Doggy 1's sister about him. I just want to check if he is serious about us or not. You know, I need to know because I can't stop thinking about him and us being together," she said in panic because she knew I would not agree to that. It was close to stalking, even if she was in love with him. She was about to humiliate herself. I really wanted to prevent that.

"I get it, but chasing him is not going to make him love you! Believe me, I've been there. It hurts a lot, it's personal humiliation and self-destruction. This is not the way towards love and happiness." I had my moment of honesty not only with the Witch, but it was also my personal "aha" moment. Finally, I realised what my problem regarding romantic relationships was. *"I am a giver, not a taker. I am a chaser!"* I thought to myself. I didn't feel sorry for myself. I was disappointed with myself. I wanted to know and understand why I kept doing it to myself. That was the first thought about me and my relationships. Well, it didn't last longer than a split second, and it disappeared. I was too busy with others' happiness and I didn't see that I needed that for myself. *"Nah, it would be selfish to care about myself,"* I thought and back to taking care of the Witch. I was wrong then, that is why the process of loving myself first didn't start then.

And the Witch? Nah, she didn't hear me, she didn't understand it at all. Really, she was in the mode: "Him or nobody, and the rest of the world can go and shag itself."

"Heh, girl, you are one stubborn bitch. Let's do it!" I said to her. *"Let's have some fun,"* I thought to myself.

We arrived at the village and parked far from the Doggies' house, just in case they would be back from work and notice the car. The Witch went to see Doggy 1's sister to have a heart-to-heart conversation. I went to the local pub for a glass of cranberry juice. Yeah, just juice! Well, I have always been a responsible driver. I always think about others rather than about myself. Yeah, another sign of being a "giver", right? *"I am a giver, no matter what."* I had time to myself, to think. *"Do I deserve to receive all those good things such as: honest and pure love, someone to share my fears, dreams, joy with? What did I do deserve to be the one who only serves others? Damn, how much longer will I be trapped in this state of mind? How long before I can move from this place and from this job? When will I be able to do something that I really, really deserve. I want it so much."* I was going through all of that in my head, sipping my juice while I was waiting for the Witch. Nothing revolutionary come to me, literally; nada, nothing, zero.

The Witch walked into the pub. I could see from a distance that she was pissed off. Her face was burning, she was raging, fumes were puffing out from her nostrils and ears like a bull ready to attack.

"The f*^&*) ^ with him! Get me a drink!" she shouted at me; not to me.

"OK, you got it, just a moment." I turned to the bartender, and I asked for a double whiskey and two cranberry juices. The Witch didn't drink strong alcohol, but I felt that this time she would need it. She just grabbed the shot and emptied it at once. *"Wow, she is not herself!"* I thought to myself.

"What happened?" I asked gently.

"His sister was laughing at me! Can you imagine?" she said. *"Well, yes, I could imagine that."* I was answering that in my head, not her. I also noticed her grotesque desperation as she was trying get the boy to love her. I have mentioned that fact before but at that moment, it was not the time to add miseries. *"Damn, I am feeling for her. She is a giver too!"* I reflected on my reaction.

"Oh, dear. What did she say?" I asked to let her unload her feelings.

"She said he is not interested in me. It is just a joke, fun and nothing ever will be serious between me and him. She said she knows him well, dah, like a sister, and she knows I am not his type." The Witch stopped to gasp for air. "She said that I am a good girl, but he deserves someone better!" She stopped, looked at me like a helpless puppy that needs to be rescued, and she burst into tears. *"Oh, the whiskey did its magic,"* I thought. "Let's go outside," I said. While I was almost dragging her through the door, the Doggies walked into the pub through the other door. But they didn't notice us, most importantly, she didn't see them. *"Wow, now we have a situation,"* I thought and started to make an evacuation plan in my mind. For sure, I couldn't tell her that they were in the pub.

"Listen, you've had enough for today. Let's go home. You need rest. A good sleep will help you to see things better tomorrow. Is it a good plan?" I was hoping for her approval. Nah, the Witch continued to fall apart, mainly because of the whiskey she had. She started crying more, and she didn't hear me at all. *"Damn, I can't let her go back into the pub, not like that. Think, woman!"* I was rushing myself to find a way out.

"Hey, look, it's late. We need to be at work tomorrow by 5am and The Hawk will worry about me, you and the car. Come on, girl, we will sort something out, but later, OK?" I begged her. The Witch just nodded her head and let me walk her to the car.

We drove off, and she was still sobbing, then she got hiccups, loud ones. That was a bad sign. I immediately stopped the car at the side of the road. I pushed to open her door, then pushed her through the door and she puked. She just missed the door frame. The Witch's half body was hanging over the door frame and I was holding her by her trousers belt so she wouldn't fall out on the road. The Witch finished, and I pulled her back into the car.

She was still having massive hiccups, more like convulsions. I had no water to give her, it could help to get rid of it. I drove fast to get her home before "next delivery" from her stomach. I got her home right on time. Literally she sprang out of the car like an arrow through the door and disappeared inside her house. *"OK, she is safe! It's only a wee alcohol-related disaster. She will be fine tomorrow,"* I thought, waved to her flatmate and drove off.

I got home late, but The Hawk was still up waiting for me.

"Hey, did you two have fun?" he asked in a friendly tone.

"Not really, but I don't want to talk about it." I really didn't want to talk about it. It was a personal disaster for the poor Witch.

"OK, no problem. Did you refill the car as I told the Witch to do?" he asked.

"Oh, crap, no! She didn't tell me that! Neither before we went, nor on the way home. Well, on the way back she was very upset and sick like a dog. She was so absorbed in the meeting and her expectations that she forgot." I was explaining the Witch's behaviour, hoping that he would understand.

"I don't care! I need a car to run tomorrow, with a full tank!" He was angry.

"Alright! I would do it, even now, but it's too late to get fuel anywhere! Here, take the money and sort it yourself. I will sort it with her tomorrow. OK?" I snapped. On the other hand, I did understand his reaction. He was right to be disappointed with the Witch, but with me? I was the middle man. Damn messenger, right?

"OK, OK," he growled. He took the money and disappeared into his room.

"Oh, the Witch, I will get to you tomorrow," I thought and went to bed.

The next day the Witch arrived at work pale and with a face swollen like a balloon. She could barely open her eyes to see the mushrooms on her shelf.

"Hey, how are you?" I asked gently, but I did not plan to go easy on her.

"I am not in the mood," she replied without even looking my direction.

"Well, The Hawk wasn't happy about the fuel in his car." I mentioned last night's conversation with The Hawk.

"He can go to hell. I don't care." The Witch said with anger.

"Easy tiger, I am just a messenger, so don't shout at me, alright?" I tried to calm her down.

"OK, I will give you the money for fuel later, OK?" she pleaded with me.

At that moment, another picker walked into the mushroom house. Well, it was hard to call it walking; she was swaying side to side trying to walk straight. She was well off the straight line.

"Oooo, madam! What happened to you?" I was curious.

"The hell with last night, it lasted all night long until 5am this morning!" she stated, with hiccups in between the words.

"Wow, it's only 7am now!" I told her.

"Oh, that means that I didn't sleep at all. I am still having a party!" She was dancing around her trolley.

"How are you going to make it to the top of your trolley?" I asked. I was a bit worried about her being on top of the trolley in her condition.

"Don't you worry, mama! I will be fine," she replied and went straight on the top of her trolley. The trolley made a few jerks side to side. She grabbed the side of the mushroom shelf to hold herself tight.

"I am alright! No worries!" she shouted so loud that our supervisor on the other side of the house jumped.

"Hey, dievchonka (girl) get down before you hurt yourself!" He gave the order.

"Yes, captain, I am coming down!" She vigorously saluted him, and her trolley moved forward. She lost her balance and grabbed the edge of the mushroom shelf again. She hung on to the shelf while her trolley rolled away from under her feet. It was about three meters drop from her shelf. She most definitely was not in any condition to jump from this height. She was quite a strong girl but also quite big in terms of her height and weight. Nevertheless, she held on to the structure.

"Oh, pizdiet, mayey loshadi krisha poyehala! – [f*&&, my horse went crazy!]" she shouted in Russian as she was hanging on the top shelf. She named her trolley a horse.

"Hold your shit, girl!" I shouted and ran to rescue her. I was closest to her but on the opposite side of the same shelf. I jumped off my trolley, and I pushed it toward my hanging, drunk friend. She jumped on the top of my trolley.

"Look at me, I am a crazy acrobat!" She was wobbling on the top of my trolley with her arms in the air like a winner.

"Girl, get off my trolley. You've scared the crap out of me, drunk monkey!" I was laughing at her, but I was shaking a bit inside. In my imagination, I saw her falling and breaking her neck a few seconds before.

"I am not a monkey; I am a drunk acrobat!" She was arguing back while she was climbing down.

"Yeah, yeah, whatever!" I calmed myself down.

The whole mushroom house was laughing at her and that's how she earned her nickname: "The drunk monkey". The nickname stuck with her for the rest of our time working together, and a bit longer after that.

. . . .

No doubts, most of us fell for the "false love alarm" and we paid for that severely. Our expectations were high, emotions were intense, yet the other person did not share the same feelings. **Our emotions and feelings triggered the love alarm**. The subject of our love might have had a completely different agenda. Did he/she feel the same? Did he/she want to be loved by us? Were they responsible for our emotions? When we found negative answers to those questions, the alarm of love was gone. We realised it was a false alarm and with the full speed of emotional frustration we hit the wall of disappointment. What comes next? Alcohol! That substance is incredibly dangerous when mixed with the

emotional fire of disaster, and "sprinkling" alcohol on is a dangerous game. It is definitely not a remedy for a broken heart. It leads
to self-destruction if it's not stopped. This game may be lethal.

What should you do instead? Heal your wounded soul and
broken heart with self-love. Write down all your anger, negative
thoughts and work through it fully imagining the best vendetta
plan. Just use pen and paper, of course! Vent your rage and frustration on paper. Give yourself just five minutes of fury. Then
burn the paper! Safely!

Next, Check Your Daily Exercises on how to do The Five
Minutes of Rage and The Five Seconds rule.[8]

Alcohol? In my personal opinion everything in moderation
is good for human beings. Drink alcohol wisely for happy occasions and celebrations in great company. But first, heal yourself
fully and love yourself endlessly!

---

8 The 5 seconds rule – Mel Robbins.

YOUR DAILY EXERCISES

The Five minutes of rage

We are all responsible for our emotions and our experiences. Nobody else is. Accept it here and now! Especially while we are dealing with others, our negative emotions might be triggered by their words, behaviour, etc. In some extreme situations they may "push" your ultra-sensitive button and make you snap in a millisecond. Your emotional control will swiftly go out through the window. GIVE YOURSELF A BREAK IMMEDIATELY! LEAVE THE ROOM, EVEN THE BUILDING!

You need to release the pressure; you need to get rid of those destroying emotions from your entire system, for you and others, safely and completely. Push your whole frustration through physical rage just for 5 minutes, not a minute longer, by doing one or more of the following:

- Scream at the top of your lungs. Try not to scare anyone.
- Stamp hard, even jump if you feel like it.
- Clench your fists, but do not punch anything and/or anyone. You don't need criminal offence records. Or physical harm on your body. No!
- Cry, puke.
- Run in a circle.
- Wash your face with cold water.
- Or any other physical method you know that is safe but works for you.

Remember, you have only 5 minutes. Set the timer!

Or less physical rant:

- Write down all your thoughts and emotions on paper. No matter how many pages you fill with your anger, stress, disappointment, fury, resentment, write it all down. The paper will take everything! Just remember, you only have 5 minutes to do so. Set the timer. Then rip it up, bin it, wash your face.

No matter which method you use to get you out of your brain, do it for only 5 minutes. Then stop and use the 5 seconds rule (below) to completely focus on your breathing. First, breath out all the air, next deep breath in, repeat it 6 times. With your sixth breath in... use the 5 seconds rule again to move on. It works like a total reset for your brain. Brings calmness and allows you to regain emotional control.

The Five Seconds Rule by Mel Robbins

Mel Robbins wrote a book about how she discovered the 5 seconds rule. The idea is brilliant and as simple as counting 5, 4, 3, 2, 1 and switching your negative thought into a positive one. For example: you had a bad day, you start ruminating on all the daily events in your head. Immediately, all your negative emotions appear. STOP HERE and NOW! Start counting down 5, 4, 3, 2, 1 and think about something completely different and pleasant: "I am taking a bath." Have a home spa, watch stand-up comedy, funny animals on YouTube, do anything that makes you feel happy, loved and safe.

You can use the Five seconds rule as often as you need! With this exercise, you won't need the five minutes of rage!

2.8 THE SQUIRREL

In the meantime, having a full support of our bosses, the Squirrel was "cooking" his plan behind our backs.

We worked like a farmer's donkey, 7 to 10 days in a row. Each shift was at least 14 hours long with a brief break of 15 to 20 minutes for some food and toilet. How had we managed through each day of the labour camp on the mushroom farm? Well, I am not entirely sure myself, but we managed.

I felt like I was hanging there, between getting out of bed at 4.30am and back to bed at 11pm. I was half-conscious and in half-lethargic state of mind with repetitive, automatic movements. Literally, there were moments when I have lost count of days. We were all exhausted to the point that we could've dropped dead.

The Squirrel called a meeting of all pickers, and he dropped the "bomb".

"So, I would like all of you to start a shift at 4am," he stated without hesitation.

Everyone was holding their breaths and their eyeballs were about to pop out of their faces. Including my own. *"Are you for real? Are you out of your mind?"* Those questions were pounding in my mind.

Everyone peered at our team leader who pretended that she was not there. *"Holly, molly, she knew!"* I realised instantly. *"You, f*^R%^ bitch, you knew, you sold us, traitor!"* I thought. My blood was boiling but someone had to speak up.

"It would be difficult for most of us. You know that some of us are living an hour drive from here and the taxi driver is not exactly good at time keeping." I tried to reason with the Squirrel.

"Well, it's not my business how you get here. As for you, I know that you have moved nearby, so others can do the same, right?" he answered. He was as cool, as a cucumber.

"Not really. They have families." I was pleading, but I had nothing more to add.

The Squirrel was holding a straight face; he did not move a muscle, a total poker face.

"Do you want us to start our shift in the middle of the night? When should we get some sleep?" I asked.

"Well, it's entirely up to you ladies, but I just want you to know that soon I will have a team of pickers who will pick mushrooms in the middle of the night." He said that without any emotions, like he was delivering a report on the livestock. Just numbers, emotionless info. *"Fricking sociopath!"* This was pumping in my head.

Then the moment of doubt appeared. *"Hold on, who are those people? Are they dumber than we are?"* Those thoughts ran through my mind in a split second. How naive was I? Well, let's say I was an example of positive thinking. As always, I saw the glass half full.

"Aha, good, so that would be more help for us?" I asked naively.

"I am not sure if you are going to be happy with this kind of help, but we will see about that." He delivered his statement, and he tried to walk out.

"What do you mean, that they wouldn't be a help to us?" I was trying to understand our position.

"Well, until all mushroom houses are in full production stage there might be a shortage of mushrooms for everyone. Which means that you will make less money for some time, but I cannot tell you for how long." The Squirrel was honest at least.

"Is he saying that we will need a new job?" My brain was processing thousand thoughts per second. *"I don't have a visa. I don't have savings. I don't have connections to get a visa. The small town I am living in has no jobs for illegal migrants with minimum language. I am in shit up to my ears!"* My fear was growing. I already saw a disaster of being homeless, deported, and humiliated! The pointer on my emotional map jerked to fear and anxiety. *"Damn, there has to be something else for me here."* There was only one hopeful thought I was trying to hang on to. At that very moment, it was just hope. My mind tried to hold on to that hope, but it was too tiny and weak. I still tried to be reasonable.

"So, how much time do we have to prepare for the new arrangements?" I asked.

"A few weeks. I will let you know near the time." His answer did not satisfy me at all. The Squirrel ended the meeting and walked out of the canteen like it was another appraisal meeting.

Everyone was confused, mainly because they did not understand English, and some rough translations were still being done. Of course, the more information they were getting, the more questions were coming. Everyone was looking for our team leader, but she vanished. With my best intentions and loads of practice in the Russian language, I explained the issue to those who understood Russian. The Russian speakers translated into Lithuanian and Latvian. The Czech guys were waiting for a Polish version from me. The air in the canteen was thick with despair, hopelessness, and helplessness.

Nobody knew what to expect next, and nobody dared to even ask that question out loud. We all went home feeling like beaten dogs with tails between our legs.

I went home with The Hawk and Sloth. The silence in the car was suffocating. The Hawk parked the car outside our door. Without a single word, the three of us went straight into the bar under our apartment. Our communication was transcendent and unanimous. We needed a drink. I ordered tequila shots and pints of beer. The bartender was not surprised at all; he adored my tequila bravery.

The Czechs and I were sitting in silence for some time, just enjoying the drinks.

"I was in a library the other day to use the Internet and I saw a job advert for a butcher in The Big Town," the Hawk said. "It's over an hour's drive from here, and money is good, too," he continued.

I looked at him like he was from another planet. "What it has to do with our situation, my situation to be exact?" I did not see the point at all. I knew that The Hawk was a butcher and Sloth could have some useful skills, too. But me? The closest I have been to anything related with a butcher was when I went shopping and occasionally disembowelled a chicken before cooking it. So?

"Pshonka, you are retarded! If they need butchers, they might need packers too!" The Hawk looked at me with disappointment.

"Aha…, you are right, I can do packing, no problem. But there is a wee, tiny problem. I am illegal!" Those last three words came out so loud that even the bartender turned his head towards us.

"Shuh you!" the Hawk yelled at me. Sloth just rolled his eyes.

"Look, I will call them. It's a small family company. I can ask if they will take you without papers." The Hawk was really helping and thinking ahead. He had been planning to move there for a few weeks already. He decided to share his plans only because of that meeting with the Squirrel. I was speechless, then downed my tequila shot.

"Oh, you cheeky bastard, you didn't say a word about it." Sloth, who was usually mute, exploded. Then he downed his tequila shot. The Hawk, with a big smile on his face, joined us with his shot.

"I didn't say anything not to raise false hopes for myself, you, and also for her. I called them last week. I am going to see the boss on Monday, next week." The Hawk couldn't stop himself from grinning as he watched us stare at him like he was a miracle maker.

"Beautiful, congratulations! You won the competition for the most secretive and cruel companion ever!" I said. It was painfully shocking to me that he didn't tell me about his plans, as we were honest and open towards each other.

"Pshonka, you don't get it. Before I will share anything with others and the world, I do some research first, just in case it would fail. Then only I would know that it failed, and nobody would call me a liar and failure," the Hawk explained like I was a four year old child.

It made sense. He was protecting himself from being judged by anyone. The Hawk was totally different. I would tell the whole world about my plans, big ideas, just to share my joy of creative thinking. However, there was always a bunch of critics, judges, who were waiting for my failures, that gave them something to talk about. Today I know that it had nothing to do with me and my life, only their lives were sad and empty. My attempts, positive or not were lighting up their lives with excitement they've missed so much. They found my attempts with negative outcomes especially delightful. The lodge of mockers with full right for judgement. Although, I didn't know back then that all my failures were valuable lessons. The one thing I should do instead of crying and raging, was to pay attention to those lessons, reflect on them to protect myself on every level as I moved on. It's never too late for that. Watch me!

We were still at the bar. The Hawk's grin was getting bigger with every shot. Sloth was getting more vocal with every shot. I was getting more grateful for my Czech Angels who were willing to rescue me. My thankfulness grew with every shot. The little light at the end of the tunnel had just appeared.

After a few drinks, with a lighter sense of being, we went upstairs to our apartment. We sat with beers in the living room. Our flatmate, called The Cat for his gentle personality, appeared at the door and asked us what was wrong with The Hen? He reported that The Hen came into the house like a tornado with two big shopping bags filled with alcohol and locked herself in her room without a single "Hello". He was not impressed with The Hen, but he was genuinely worried about her.

The Cat also worked on our mushroom farm. In fact, he was kind and gentle towards everybody. However, he was the right hand and shadow of the Squirrel. The Squirrel brought The Cat with him from previous employment. Frankly speaking, for that reason, we were a bit reluctant towards him.

Until today. The Cat had a day off, so he was really surprised to hear about the meeting. The Hawk was watching him closely while he was telling him about the Squirrel's plans. The Cat said that there were some rumours about new pickers, but he was too busy to listen. His job was to load the pallets on the lorry and he was working alone that day. The Hawk was still staring at him like he could X-ray him searching for the truth. The Cat sensed Hawk's intentions.

"Come on, I am not a snitch. Sure, as hell not for the Squirrel! If I knew that was something important, I would have listened. The lorry was late, and I had to hurry up to finish on time." The Cat was trying to convince The Hawk.

"Oy, stop it, he is telling the truth. I was there. Well, I mean I didn't hear it, but I saw him working like crazy on his own many times." I tried to ease the pressure.

"Yeah, but it does not mean he didn't know about it, or the Squirrel did not talk to him on any other occasion." It looked like The Hawk had lost his trust in The Cat.

"Mhm... he is right, so would you be so kind as to be honest with us?" I pleaded with The Cat.

"For real, guys, this is the first time I hear about it, now!" He was ready to swear on his own life.

"I believe him," I said with full confidence. The Hawk was still reluctant, and Sloth was giving his full approval with nodding.

At this moment, The Hen showed up behind The Cat's back. *"I knew, I f& (*& knew it!"* The Hen shouted straight into the Cat's ear. He jumped.

"Oh, here is our hero!" I yelled. I was loud, but I wasn't angry loud, just tipsy! The Hen burst into tears."

"The Squirrel is a damn bastard, he told me all about it, and then he made me swear to keep it a secret." The Hen cried. She was drunk as hell. She couldn't even stand on her feet. Then she collapsed on her bum, still holding her bottle with drink in it. The Cat went down to rescue her, but she pushed him away to leave her alone. The Cat, completely helpless, stood above her and looked at us, awaiting some instructions.

"Leave her there. She had enough," The Hawk advised him.

"Well, what are we going to do with our wee traitor?" I asked just out of curiosity. I was not in the mood to deal with her, my anger was long gone.

"I think she is punishing herself already," The Hawk stated. Sloth nodded in agreement. The Cat, still unsure whether to leave her on the floor or not was hanging above her head. Eventually, The Cat just waved at us and vanished to his room. I was tired of work issues, drunk, and emotionally exhausted by all those events. It was a bit too much for one person.

We all went to our rooms, except The Hen who was still sitting on the floor in the living room, sobbing and drinking Later, I heard her getting up from the floor, swearing out loud in her own language. I think she bumped into her door, but I didn't check on her. I was falling asleep.

Next morning, we were all up, getting ready for work, except The Hen. I knocked on her door, but there was no answer. "Well, she is an adult. She knows better. It is her decision," I said to the others.

The atmosphere at the mushroom farm, was like at a funeral. No chatting, no laughing, no comments, just work. The Irish ladies were not aware of the meeting with the Squirrel, as it happened long after they finished work.

Mousey was the one who tried to communicate as she could understand our pidgin English and she would usually chat with me. Mousey asked me what was going on. When I explained as clear as I could she went: "No f *&^*&^ way! It's not fair!" I was astonished by her reaction.

"Not fair indeed. Now, not fair for whom, the Irish or the others?" I had no mercy because we were treated differently all the time, and that was no secret.

"On all of us, of course! To me there is no difference. We are all pickers here!" Mousey was genuinely raging. "I was even fighting with my husband, who was commanding me to stop speaking to him with 'a Russian accent', he said. And I told him to get lost. I will speak as I like and the way my friends speak to me." All of us pickers who could understand English reacted instantly, we started cheering, clapping our hands and rejoicing together. We were astonished at her speech. For the first time we felt like a team, despite the difference in the way were treated, employment statuses, nationalities, age and many others.

The cheering was so loud that it alarmed the Squirrel and The Cat who arrived at the mushroom house, curious what was going on. Literally, they were ignored by the whole team. None of us was bothered to explain why we were so happy. They left, clueless.

The mood and spirit had shifted for the rest of the day. We felt stronger together!

On the same day, at home, I went to check on The Hen. I knocked on her door, but there was no answer. I could see the light coming from her room, so I let her be. Later, The Cat checked on her and she said through the door to leave her alone, so he did. Judging by her voice, she was drunk. There was nothing else we could do. The Cat asked her if she would come to work next day, but she didn't answer.

"I am worried about her," said The Cat. The worry was genuine, and I was worried about her too.

"Look, me too, but she is an adult, and she knows what she is doing. If she would like and accept our help, she would come out. We cannot force her, unfortunately." My intuition was right. By that time I already knew what her problem was, although she never admitted being an alcoholic, never to me, or anybody else, never to herself. That's the nature of this illness.

We didn't have work for two days. The Hawk and Sloth went to meet the boss in The Big Town and ask for a job for me too. In the meantime, one of our bosses came into our house to check on The Hen. She was on a drinking spree for four days already. It was too much for all of us at home.

"We need her to get sober. We need her at the farm," *The boss said.*

"What has that got to do with me? What about work for me?" I asked, a bit annoyed. It was a bit too much for me. He came to me and asked me to fix the Hen, but he didn't worry about me and how I was going to survive. Why? Ah... I am illegal. She had a visa. Yeah, that's a massive difference. I said to him that I would try to help her. Although, I never said that I would do it for him and the farm. I wanted to help her, because she was a human, a lost human, an ill human who will possibly never admit that she needs help. The boss left without answering my question.

Only two of us were at home at that time, so I prepared a cold bath for her. I knocked on her door, she answered, and I went inside. WOW! I had never seen so many bottles in the one room. The floor was totally covered with every possible bottle that contained alcoholic drink. The full range of alcohols available in off licence shops. The Hen was half-awake and on the edge of delirium. I dragged her to the bathroom and chucked her into the cold water. She was squealing like a pig but sat in the water for a good 15 minutes. In the meantime, I cleaned up her room, taking out all empty, half-empty and full bottles. I opened the windows to get some fresh air, stripped her bed and made a fresh one. The Hen got out of the bath frozen like a piece of ice, chattering her teeth and shivering like a leaf. I made her chicken soup and a big cup of tea. The Hen survived only three spoons of the soup and threw up. She was really sick. Every single non-alcoholic liquid was escaping her body. Her system was clearing itself. A few hours later, she could handle a piece of bread in her stomach.

The Hawk and Sloth returned from The Big Town. They were quite happy about the job, but the job was only for them. The boss offered them an immediate start and accommodation in one of his houses. There was no place for me, not yet, anyway. The Hawk promised to keep talking to the boss about me.

"Well done, boys. I am happy for you!" I was truly happy for them. I also knew that they were not happy to leave me behind. "When are you going then?" I asked.

"In two days. I will talk to our bosses here to get our papers ready. I hope he will get them ready in two days. If not, well, we will go anyway and come back later for papers and for you." The Hawk tried to smile to cheer me up.

"No worries, I will be here because there is no work now at the farm. Well, none for me anyway." I told them about the boss' visit and his desperation for The Hen to be sobered up, and all those legal/illegal games.

"Once we have the house in The Big Town, we will take you there with or without a job. You can't stay here!" The Hawk declared his support. The three of us declared to keep it secret.

"Alright then, I will sit tight here and wait for your call." I felt relief already, even if I had to wait a few weeks for that call. *"I will survive. Everything will work out for me."* My mind was hooked on that mantra.

The Hen came into the living room to announce that me and her were going to work tomorrow. Then she turned around and went straight into her bedroom. The Hen didn't mention work for The Hawk and Sloth, but they didn't worry at all. They had their own plans, anyway.

Next morning, The Hen took me and The Cat to work like nothing happened. The past four days did not happen at all. *"Fair enough, you don't need to thank me, you don't need to look after me. I will survive."* I thought on the way.

It was a day like many others at the farm, until lunchtime. The Hen vanished from the farm again. The Squirrel was "flying" up and down checking something at the back of the farm. The work was hard as usual. There were a few houses to clear up and no time for a break.

It was the middle of November, so after 4pm it was dark outside. There were a few lampposts on the farm, but it was still hard to see anything in the distance.

The Squirrel told us to change house, but he also changed the order of the houses, so we were at the front of the farm. I went to the canteen for a hot drink before I changed house and then I saw something strange was going on at the back of the farm. I was peering through the darkness, and I tried to figure out what it was. *"I will be damned!"* I whispered to myself, and I ran to the mushroom house to tell the others about my discovery.

"Wow, girls! There are two mobile homes parked at the back of the farm!" I yelled at the door, but in Russian so The Squirrel wouldn't understand even if he could hear me.

"What do you mean? What mobile homes? Are we moving here?" All the girls were shouting at the same time.

"I don't know, go and see for yourself. Just be careful. The Squirrel might be somewhere there," I told them. A few girls went there pretending that they needed the toilet, canteen, etc.

They came back confused with the same report: mobile houses were at the back of the farm. *What the hell?*

The Cat appeared at our mushroom house, and we knew that he had a soft spot for one of our young pickers so we encouraged her to ask him what was going on there. The Cat was shocked that she wanted to talk to him as she never did before. The girl was young, innocent, and inexperienced, so she went straight to the point. The Cat immediately got what was going on and remained tight-lipped. *"Damn, she has no diplomacy skills whatsoever,"* I thought. Well, it will come out at some point, but curiosity was stronger than ever. *"OK Cat, I will get you at home."* I thought to myself.

There were more surprises awaiting at home.

First of all, The Hawk and Sloth reported that The Hen moved out. They had no clue where she went. The Hen totally ignored their questions and didn't even say goodbye to them.

Secondly, The Hawk and Sloth went to the farm, but the bosses, including the Squirrel were too busy to even pay attention to their resignation and paperwork request. They just sent them to the office to sort it out, without any thank you, good luck or goodbye. In fact, the lady at the office sorted their documents on the spot. The Hawk and Sloth were ready to go to The Big Town. They were waiting for the new boss to confirm their accommodation. WOW! The speed of the events made me feel a bit dizzy.

At last, I told them about the discovery at the back of the farm while The Cat was in the kitchen. The three of us joined him there.

"Right, we know that you know what is going on there!" I started without any warning.

"What do I know?" The Cat played his game, but he couldn't keep a straight face. "Do I know about The Hen? Yeah, I know. She moved to the other farm, and she is still team leader there." He dropped the bomb.

I thought that I had hearing and understanding problems at the same time. HOW?

"You are kidding me, right? She was f*^*&^% drunk for four days, not showing up for work and they offered her the same job? Did they give her super-worker bonus too?" I was raging. Seriously, there was no justice, no equality, no fairness in the whole world.

"I don't know about any bonus, but she keeps her job over there." The Cat said that with a bit of bitterness on his face. Evidently, he was disgusted, too.

"Whatever, damn I wish her well, anyway. Now, you know what I am asking about. What is going on at the back of the farm?" I tossed away The Hen subject like a hot potato.

The Cat looked at me, then at the Czechs. He gave a big sigh like he was preparing for the confession of his life. "I bet you sent that girl to me today, didn't you?" He tried to skip the confession.

"Come on, don't play that stupid game, please," I pleaded with him.

"OK, the rumour is that new pickers are on the way straight from Asia and they will stay at the back of the farm." He said that slowly with a deep sadness in his voice and another big sigh at the end. The Cat knew about modern slavery, human trafficking, and victims of forced labour. He knew more than he was saying. I didn't know back then what it was, but I could sense his reluctance immediately.

"Holly Molly..." I couldn't say anything else. "Are they going to live in those mobile houses there? During the winter?" I had hundreds of questions running through my head. The Hawk and Sloth were sitting in silence. Their jaws dropped to the floor.

The Cat just nodded his head but refused to answer any more questions. He swiftly changed the subject. "I hear that you two are leaving. Is that true?" The Cat pointed at The Hawk and Sloth. The Hawk's freeze mode wore off immediately.

"Yeah, we are moving out tomorrow to The Big Town," The Hawk answered.

"Oh, so nice. I wish you both all the best!" The Cat said politely. He turned to me: "So now it will be only two of us here, so romantic!" He laughed. For the record, there was nothing romantic or anything of the sort going on between us, just co-workers and flatmates.

"Oh, yes, we will have dinners for two at home, hahahaha."
I laughed artificially.

"Superb, I can see the two of you holding hands and sharing pitta bread." The Hawk laughed. Sloth chortled to the idea. I shot them with 'a killer' look. If looks could kill, both of them would've been dead by then." Instead, I changed the subject.

"Well, our last night flatmates! Let's celebrate the endings and new beginnings!" I called for drinks. I have brought a few bottles of beer I've confiscated from The Hen. It was for her good and our health. We stayed up and chatted late that night, making jokes about our time together at that house. The good, the bad, the naughty, the ugly and the funniest moments. An ordinary bunch of friends who made some great memories for life.

I was and still am grateful for all those people in my life. All those lessons, experiences and memories are still vivid in my mind. It was, though, an emotional roller-coaster with no predictions available, not even hints of the upcoming future. From sweet, innocent happiness through powerlessness, hopelessness into the dark miserable hole of anxiety. No light at the end of the tunnel.

We shared the power of true friendship, The Cat, The Hawk, Sloth and I. Our friendship helped us to survive and strive in our own way. Even The Hen with her dark secret of illness had her positive influence on me. The Hen had shown me who I don't want to be at any stage of my life.

I knew that I could count on my Czechs. That was really sweet and it was a relief for me. They knew that I would go to hell and back for them. It was simple support with mutual respect.

As for The Cat, he had his own plans for life, and that was his sweet secret. The mushroom farm was his first step towards the future. Did he achieve his goals? I really don't know, but I hope he did.

We all knew that our bright new future was just unfolding for us. There were only two things we didn't know: when and how. But as for myself, I accepted the Marvellous Time and Plan to unfold it.

. . . .

Be grateful for everything and everyone in your life. No matter the feelings the lesson triggers in you, keep THINKING POSITIVELY! Yeah, I know. I've been there! It's hard, it's painful, and feels like it lasts for eternity. Those were my thoughts, too. And I have managed to change them! You can do it too. I believe in you, just try and try again.

Do you remember the 5 seconds rule? Yes? Good, so 5,4,3,2,1, "I love myself. I am grateful for my life. I am safe." Repeat, over and over and breathe.

2.9 THE SILENCE BEFORE THE STORM

The next few days were interesting. I watched those events like an observer from the distance. All my emotions were numb, covered with a thick layer of "*I don't care*". My brain was hooked on my mantra, not allowing any emotional signals to come to the surface of consciousness. My body was functioning in auto-mode: work, eat, drink, sleep, repeat. Entirely robotic functioning.

The Hawk and Sloth were already in The Big Town. We made regular calls in the evenings. Usually, The Hawk called to keep me posted about the job and to complain about Sloth just being himself. They were already like an old married couple, so their quarrels made me laugh.

I was reporting the events at the farm. Two days after they left, the pickers from Asia arrived, but nobody has seen them. By nobody, I mean other pickers and ground staff. The Irish pickers were speculating about them, for example: are they in the mobile houses already? When are they going to start to work and so on? The other legal and illegal pickers were curious too, but too busy and too tired to make any comments about the new pickers. Although, the hot topic was The Hen who vanished from our farm to appear on another farm. Of course, friends have friends, and the news was sprinting between farms. Gossiping about others was a standard procedure and nothing would pass without detection and judgement. They wanted some insights from me; they knew that we were flatmates. Once again, I didn't give them that satisfaction. I remained loyal not to my former flatmate, but loyal to myself. Besides, I didn't have many details to share about The Hen moving to the other farm. Well, they were not impressed with me. That was fine with me!

On the fifth day after the new pickers arrived, we were so busy that we didn't have time for any breaks. Well, nothing unusual, but where were the new girls or boys to help? Still no sign of them and still no help.

I was walking across the yard in the middle of the day, and I heard some shouting and screaming behind me. There were at least three, maybe four voices. I jumped, a bit alarmed, and turned toward the screams; it was like a cry for help. At the back of the farm, behind the mobile houses, I saw a person running across the empty field and two others chasing the person. It was difficult to see if it was a girl or boy, from the distance. I couldn't recognise the chasers either.

The other voices were coming from mobile houses like they were cheering the runner. I stood there, in the middle of the yard, and watched that scene like in a movie. I was not able to understand what I was looking at. Back then I didn't know about human trafficking and modern slavery at all. Moreover, I didn't know that I was a victim of forced labour for years until I got to the University, seventeen years later.

Back to the scene, I was watching the chase emotionlessly. After maybe ten seconds the two chasers reached the runner and pushed him or her to the ground. The cheering at the mobile houses stopped immediately. Two chasers lifted the runner and, holding the person's arms walked together towards the mobile houses. There was a person near the mobile houses, it was a woman who was shouting out some orders in a foreign language. The woman was dressed and behaved differently than the others. I didn't know what her role was, but it looked like she was some kind of a guard or supervisor. The tone she was using to shout orders sounded more like "barking" through the teeth. That sound made the other girls move obediently, like soldiers.

The chasers brought the runner into one of the mobile houses and went inside together. There was no more screaming or shouting, but a very unpleasant silence.

Then I felt that something was not right. My intuition was screaming inside me, but I couldn't read it properly then. One of our pickers called my name and that unfroze me. My intuition stopped calling, and I went to work like nothing happened. I didn't say a word to the others about what I saw. The whole incident entirely disappeared from my mind immediately. Automatically, I switched to my auto-mode again.

Later that night, I was talking to The Hawk. Then I retrieved the incident from my memory. My intuition started shouting again, and again I didn't recognise the nudge. I told The Hawk about the incident. The Hawk was laughing like I was talking about some comedy show. But I had that disturbing picture and sound in my memory, it didn't feel funny at all.

Of course, the others and me, we were complaining about long hours of work with no breaks. We were complaining to each other and to The Squirrel. The Squirrel said nothing, but he had the smirk on his face with an expression of "you don't know what is coming."

"Asshole!" I thought to myself, as I didn't like his facial expression at all. It gave me creeps. I could sense his diabolic intentions. Yes, it was my intuition! We didn't have to wait much longer, just two more days!

Two days later, we arrived at the farm around 5am. We went to the last house we left on the day before to finish the harvest. It was clear! Clear, zero, null, nada, all mushrooms were picked. The whole process of growing mushrooms was divided into three stages called flash. All mushrooms picked from the first flash, then the next flash will show up in three, four days. The third flash usually was the last. If that was the last flash, then the mushroom bedding would have been changed completely and the new flash would come up in a week or so.

Last night we left at least half of the house to be picked in the morning. What the hell? Nah, those mushrooms did not pick and pack themselves. That magic does not exist... so? THE NEW PICKERS! They were picking our mushrooms in the middle of the night! The curse of The Squirrel just appeared in front of our eyes, just as he promised. *"DAMN YOU, EVIL SQUIRREL!"*

We went to check the next house, which should be ready for the day, and it also was cleared. The last house was waiting for the final clear. There was not much left to pick, and it was not even worth doing it. The new pickers left only rubbish for us. We couldn't make any money that day. We were fuming, raging, and cursing in all known languages. Those of us who had work permit were disappointed. The rest of us, illegal pickers, including me, we were scared. We had no rights to be in Ireland and no rights to work. What about us? Nobody cared.

Oh, yes, that was part two of The Squirrel's curse. It was too early in the morning to find someone to talk to us. Bosses and The Squirrel started work at 8.30am. It was too much for many of us to sit and wait there for three hours to see The Squirrel's smirk. I could imagine the evil expression on his face, and that was enough for me. Some pickers had their own transport, others shared transport. The rest was living within walking distance, including me. The team made the decision to go home and call the bosses later.

I left a message in the canteen for the Irish pickers who were coming later anyway, that we went home because there was no work for us that day. Well, there was no work for them either. Although, bosses had the courtesy to call them and let them know. I found out about that much later.

I sent a text to The Hawk that I desperately needed a job, or just move out of here without a job. *"I need to get out of here, now, please!"* That desperate thought was repeatedly playing in my mind.

The following few days felt like my life was on standby. The mushroom bosses didn't bother to answer my calls. There was no news from The Hawk and Sloth except that they were busy and tired. The Cat was working every day, and he had little time after work to babysit me. Frankly, there was nobody for me.

Honestly, at that time I felt and thought that the time stopped and the Earth was standing still. Everything was put on pause. There was nothing certain and I could see absolutely nothing positive at that time. There was no sign of any movement at all. *"Damn, where is the light?"* I couldn't find a single positive thought to bring the light I needed. My faith was not there either. I felt lonely and helpless.

"I could go back home" it was a fair thought. Unfortunately there was nothing waiting for me at home, not to mention the important fact - I didn't have money for a return ticket. I also didn't have work there, no home, no boyfriend, except a few friends and my mother. It was similar there to over here. With one difference, at home I was legal, but without entitlement to any benefits. In other words, same s&*^ different location and rights.

"What else can I do?" I was trying really hard to find one positive thought, single light in the tunnel, hope. Every day I walked around the small town looking for signs. Every day I stopped at the church and cried my eyes out. Not that I was a God-fearing person or strong believer, not at all. The church gave me the peaceful space to unload my emotions. Once I released those negative emotions, my inner being was coming out to calm me down with, "Everything always works out for me". Only then was I able to reflect on my past experiences, how I managed through them, survived and rose again against all odds. Only then was I able to recognise my strengths and power of positive thinking. *"Everything is temporary, the dark times will pass, and the bright ones will come again."* I tried to comfort myself. Although, the stagnation was poking holes in my very limited patience.

For over a week, I was in those mood swings from deep anxiety in the morning, through positive focusing in the afternoon and calming waves in the evening. Just surviving another day.

Then the call from The Hawk came and broke down the doubting cycle.

"Hey, pshonka, pack your bags. We are taking you to The Big Town tomorrow," The Hawk announced over the phone. I could hear the joy in his voice. He was truly happy for me to join them.

"How, what?" I couldn't speak. I was still processing his words.

"Oy, come on! Tomorrow I will come to pick you and all your things up around 6pm. Our Boss, "The Fox", agreed to give you a job and the accommodation. You will live with us." The Hawk said.

"Tomorrow? You see, I have plans for tomorrow..." I said slowly. I was teasing him.

"What plans? Do you hear me? You have a job and place to live!" The Hawk exclaimed, astonished that I dared to decline the offer. He didn't get my joke.

"Alright! No need to yell at me. I was joking!" I laughed, cried, and screamed like a little child.

"Pshonka! You scared the crap out of me! For a second, I thought that you were serious, and that you didn't want to come here." There was relief in The Hawk's voice.

"Well, here I have no work, no boyfriend, no friends except The Cat, no way out, no money. What plans could I have? No worries, I will be ready by noon and wait patiently for you," I said, and tears were rolling down my face. Tears of happiness and relief, finally.

The Cat came home from work and by just one look at me he knew that something happened. I didn't give him a chance to ask, I just blasted at him.

"I am going to The Big Town tomorrow! For good!" I cried. Then I realised that it might hurt him. "I am sorry, I just realised that you are going to be completely alone here." I looked into The Cat's eyes.

"Oh, don't be silly! I am happy for you and glad that you are moving there. You will have something better than over here. Of course, I will miss you, my friend, but you were so miserable over the past weeks that I couldn't stand watching you like that." The Cat looked into my eyes while he was saying that. I knew he was honest, and it melted my heart.

"No worries. I will be happy on my own. I don't think it will be long," The Cat paused.

"What do you mean?" I asked automatically.

"I heard today that The Hen is coming back to our farm and possibly moving back here," The Cat said with sadness in his voice.

"Oh, no! Are you sure? Maybe she will get some other place to stay?" I was surprised.

"Hmm, it doesn't look like it, but we will see. Anyway, I am happy for you! Let's have dinner and watch a movie. What do you say? Our last night, hah..." The Cat started walking towards the kitchen. "I will cook my favourite meal for you," The Cat announced with a big smile.

The Cat was a truly good cook and great companion. We had so much laughter, like the other night when the Czechs were leaving. The Cat promised to keep me posted about The Hen, and if she would be back at the house. I promised to update him on the Czechs at work and at home. Wow, that was an absolutely awesome evening!

I was so excited that I couldn't sleep. I was constantly thinking about what would happen next. That was another side of anxiety that raised my expectations. There were no promises for a great new life. I knew that I had a job and a roof over my head, that was enough. Although, my imagination was raising my expectations. My thoughts and emotions were on a free-fall and just flew. I have created the mental picture of my life with details of a beautiful job, a warm home filled with family and friends. In that mental picture there was a man, my friend, partner, lover, husband. The man with whom I would share worries, happiness, the good and the bad. Somebody I could trust, be loved and understood by. I have created a mental picture of the end of my illegal life and slavery. I made a wish for freedom of being.

I could feel that excitement rushing through my mind and body. That happy feeling pushed away my fear to the back of my mind, but not far enough. The little, annoying rascal, my inner critic was still making a sound of doubt. *"Shut your nasty mouth,"* I thought. *"You have no right to damage my dreams. You are not real."* I have tried to quench it. I focused so hard on my positive thoughts, the feel of joy, to shut down the voice of fear. Those positive thoughts helped me to push away the fear but they increased my expectations. *"Balance, woman! Find the damn balance!"* I kept telling myself.

I've decided to take small steps, try different things, go with the flow and look for new adventures. There was another rush of goose bumps. *"Adventure! Yes, yes, please, adventure. The Big Town, here I come."* With that thought, I fell asleep.

Someone said: *"Be careful what you wish for."*

Damn right! Dreams and wishes come through, believe me! The only "but" is that they do not present themselves as we imagined them in the first place. My advice is: be as much precise as you can while spelling out your wish. I have learnt how to be precise with dreams and wishes the hard way. My brave thought of *"adventurous go with a flow"* encountered a thousand bumps, big and small ones, and a few turns before I hit "the wall" of reality. Some of my wishes did hit me with the force that swept me off my feet. Some others presented themselves in totally opposite forms to my expectations.

Nevertheless, none of those obstacles stopped me then and there from pursuing my way to personal happiness.

. . . .

Never ever stop believing in your dreams, hope and help! You have the power of creation within you.

You have already learnt about the power of positive thinking here, USE IT! You have learnt about the power of visualisation, USE IT NOW! You have learnt about mindfulness, bring it into your FOCUS NOW!

Be patient and trust that everything is happening for a reason and at the right time. Just remind yourself: "Everything is working out for me! I am safe!"

YOUR DAILY EXERCISES

Quick refocus exercise

When you feel overwhelmed by your emotions and you cannot focus on anything, you need to quiet your mind. Start with a slow breath out with a breath in. Close your eyes. Breathe normally. Start slowly and count backwards from 60 to 1. Keep your focus on numbers and ignore any thoughts that might appear, just numbers. When you get to number 1, open your eyes and pick ONLY ONE task you want to complete.

CHAPTER 3

THE BIG TOWN, HERE I COME!

Next evening, The Hawk came to pick me up. There was nobody to say goodbye. The Cat was still at work, so I sent him a message that I am gone. Once we got all my things in The Hawk's car, I slammed the door and promised myself never to look back.

During over sixty kilometres drive we didn't talk much, The Hawk was too tired for a regular chat. Millions of questions were buzzing inside me. I had to control my mouth to ask only one question at the time. The only answer I got from The Hawk was, "You will see pshonka." The Hawk cut me out.

"I will, no doubt." I promised myself. I was excited, so full of positive energy that it was difficult to sit in the car.

Upon arrival, Sloth was waiting for us with lager. Sloth helped me to get my things from the car. The Hawk simply collapsed on the sofa and demanded food. The Sloth served him his meal, then gave me a tour of the house. Boom, reality revealed itself.

The bedroom they held for me was the size of a utility room at the back of a house. It was cold, dark with a tiny window with the view on the stone fence and two black bins. The bedroom could fit in a single bed and one chair, but nothing else. *"Good for me."* I tried to convince myself. *"Take it and be grateful."* Another not convincing thought. It was the best I could think there and then.

"Uhhhh, that's something else," I said out loud. "Not that I was expecting any luxury," I explained to Sloth who looked at me a bit confused.

"Pshonka! Come here!" The Hawk yelled from the living room. I moved to straddle over my bags, trying to keep my balance. Sloth already shuffled his legs to the living room.

"She doesn't like it," Sloth reported to The Hawk.

"Look, we don't have much here. The place is crap from the bottom to the top but it is cheap and that's enough for now," The Hawk explained calmly.

"I have no doubt about that," I said that with a poker face, trying to shake off initial shock. That was pure experience of contrast between expectations and reality. Boom! *"What now? What choice do I have? How long will I need to survive here?"* I was lost in my thoughts. I didn't hear a single word what The Hawk was saying about his room until he spelt out his offer.

"... so you know, you can share a room with me. It is warm, dry and clean. The only thing is, it's a double bed and no space for an extra bed there. If you feel like you can sleep with me in the same bed without having sex and fun, you are welcome." The Hawk finished and was looking at me with two big question marks in his eyes.

I was astonished by his offer, almost mesmerised. His words finally reached the right destination in my brain – "Click" or a Big "Aha" moment showed up. We have been accused of being lovers before and we both knew then and now that nothing physical would happen between us!

I looked at him, smiled softly and said: "Of course I will sleep in the same bed with you."

"Great, but if you snore, I will kick you out." The Hawk laughed. I laughed. Only Sloth was still processing what had just happened.

"You two are crazy! I don't want to hear any sex noises!" Sloth exclaimed. Me and The Hawk, we just lost it. I was laughing so hard that I fell to my knees on the living room floor. Tears of mixed emotions, relief and joy were rolling down my face. The Hawk was crawling in laughter on the sofa, trying to catch his breath. About thirty seconds later, Sloth joined us once he finally got it.

We got ourselves together after a few minutes of an uninterrupted laughter. I moved a few of my bags upstairs into The Hawk's bedroom. It was another not so impressive bedroom but definitely bigger and better than the one prepared for me downstairs.

We talked about the most important arrangements regarding our new home. I offered to clean the house for all of us while waiting for work. The Hawk asked if I would also cook for them, but Sloth protested, simply by not having faith in my cooking skills. I didn't dispute with him. The Hawk promised to talk to the boss next day about my starting date.

We went to bed by ten o'clock. Sloth, with a big grin, wished us a very, very good night. Me and The Hawk fell on the opposite sides of the bed, and we were asleep almost instantly.

I woke up after eight o'clock in the completely dark and cold room. It took me a few minutes to convince myself to leave the warm bed. *"A few more minutes and I will be fine to get out of bed. Come on, you can do it."* I was talking loudly to myself because The Hawk and Sloth were already at work.

The speed at which I had a shower and dressed was comparable to the "Flash" character. While I was drinking coffee, I was trying to figure out how to turn up the heating at home. I went from room to room, kitchen, bathroom, backyard, but found nothing that was even remotely close to a heating system. In the backyard, I found a few empty gas bottles. *"I need to keep moving constantly or I will freeze here before they come back from work."* I kept talking myself, out loud.

I decided to clean up first, then go for a walk to see the town and do some food shopping.

Let me remind you that it was an era of mobile phones with only basic functions: calls, text messages, alarm clock, and a Snake game. A fancier one could take a picture in decent resolution, but that was a luxury for those with fat pay cheques, not for a former mushroom picker, butcher, etc. So, finding an address, direction to the town centre in the new area required scout skills. We were all using real paper road maps then!

Thankfully, I have always had a good sense direction and a photographic memory for faces and places.

I went to the town centre, following the road signs and posts. I spotted a few characteristic points to find the way back home later. The town centre was not far from home, still some distance to walk, but it didn't bother me at all. I circled the centre in half an hour. *"The Big Town, the town, not so big for the county town."* I wasn't dazzled by its size, but I appreciated it much more than the villages and small towns I used to be and live in. I found the church on the main street and walked into it with a heart full of thankfulness. The church was almost empty, only a few praying people scattered around the chapel. I sat at the back, and I took a deep breath of relief. Then one more and another one before I could collect my thoughts.

"I have no words to speak how happy and grateful I am! I am so lucky to have friends like The Hawk and Sloth! Thanks to them I moved! Just a little bit, but I moved. I know that I have an opportunity to do something good for my future and I know it won't be easy, but I am here. Just one step forward, just touching the doorsteps of my future pathway. I know it will take loads of hard work to keep going. I don't care how much effort and how long it is going to take me to straighten things up, stand up and walk towards my goal, my new, better life. I am here! Thank you all for help and please keep an eye on me. In case I drift away from my new path, please just push me back on it!" I said it all in my mind, then I sat in silence for some time, and after some time I left the church. When I was walking out, my body felt lighter. My heart, my soul, and my mind felt much lighter too. It was such a relief that I could fly! For the first time in a very long time, I felt strength, confidence, and faith that everything would be good. *"Good things come to me! Everything always works out for me!"* My mantra was back. I was ready to face another challenge.

The important note here, again is, be careful and precise what you wish and/or ask for!

Well, anyway, mine was coming quickly! It was coming with a job.

. . . .

First, accept where you are right now and who you are. Use your own positive affirmation. Assure yourself that you are safe! Then go with the flow of your positive emotions and feelings towards your goal as it is already part of your reality. It is here and now already. Be precise about your thoughts. Work every detail of your dream. Each time you are imagining it make sure you are FEELING IT! Give yourself permission to feel it all, focus on its colours, smells, surroundings. How can you do it? MEDITATE! It is easier than you think! Check meditation tips after the last chapter – Your Daily Exercises!

Meditation will quieten your mind and allow you to access your inner being that holds all your higher, positive emotions, that sweet feeling of your dream as reality. Try it, it's WORTH IT!

There is an enormous power within you, so be endlessly thankful for everything here and now. Because everything always works out for you.

3.1 THE DREAM OF BACON!

Well, I've never dreamt about bacon, not voluntarily, but for the upcoming months it became my nightmare. I desperately needed work, and The Hawk was an only hope to get me one. The Hawk talked to his boss The Fox a few times. For a few weeks, The Fox's answer was "soon". The Fox – as I called the boss, had a small bacon business. He employed eight regular staff for processing meat. The other five staff, including drivers, were mainly in his office.

The company's existence and profits were based on small shops and business. Occasionally, The Fox "got" the big orders, but that happened once a year around Christmas time.

On the Irish island and across the Irish Sea, there is no English full fry without bacon! I never knew that there was such a massive requirement for bacon on both islands. The company's weekly production was tons of sliced bacon only! Small, medium, and big gammons were the only additions to the leading product. Bacon first, gammon's second. Although Christmas time was swapping that order around. Nevertheless, I had personal issues with both products.

The Christmas period was coming soon. The Fox received the "BIG" order, and he needed more people. That was a cue for me to start work.

I was physically fit after marathons on a mushroom farm, although I wasn't prepared for running with weights. Now, imagine the packing process: I was placing bags with bacon and moving the lid of the vacuum machine from side to side. All of that was done in less than thirty seconds! My colleague, who weighed those bags with bacon was unbeatable with regards to her manual speed. She was the Master of the scale! Within five minutes, she managed to create a massive pile of ready to vacuum bags of bacon. She had to stop or slow down because there was no room on the table to keep bags coming. On the other end of the bacon processing there was an industrial slicer. Although, the guy who was operating the slicer was also too slow for our Master of the scale. Then she was getting bored and annoyed with both of us.

I packed bags with bacon into boxes over twenty kilograms each. Then I ran with the full box across two rooms to the pallet outside to prepare them for delivery. On top of that I was packing different sizes of gammons, also packed into boxes of twenty kilograms each, and made them ready for delivery. I was easily doing around two thousand six hundred kilograms of lifting and running on every shift. Total gym workout!

Our first supervisor was Irish, born and raised, a family man with strong traditional principles on how to deal with work issues. He valued his skills, and he expected to be treated with respect as he respected others. He also appreciated good teamwork, simply he was fair and square with his team members. He always made sure that we were treated well by The Fox and that workload was reasonable without breaking our backs. However, The Fox ignored his requests a few times and was deaf to our supervisor's warnings that he will leave if nothing changes.

Our supervisor was an honourable man, and he stood by his words. One day he had enough of empty promises made by The Fox and he went to the office just before our first break. We went for our break without giving a single thought to what has been happened in the office. The Fox appeared in our canteen to break the news that our supervisor left the company. We were sitting there in silence and unable to chew our food with our jaws dropped to the floor. *"WHAT???!!!"* We said simultaneously. The Fox repeated the information without hesitation, then turned to "M&M", one of our butchers. We called him "M&M" short for Master and Meat. He was a highly skilled butcher.

"Can I talk to you outside, please?" The Fox asked, then stood up and went out expecting "M&M" to follow him immediately. That call totally surprised "M&M," which sounded more like an order than a request, but he went outside. The rest of us returned to chewing our food because we couldn't talk about what's just happened with our supervisor. Simply, we didn't know what happened in the office and the boss was behind the canteen door.

A few minutes passed, nothing happened, so I went for a smoke outside. Usually, "M&M" and I were going together, but he was away to the office. Well, I wanted my cigarette before returning to work.

We just returned to our workstations when "M&M" and The Fox appeared together in the work hall.

"I want your attention now. 'M&M' is your new appointed supervisor, and he is responsible for all daily orders." The Fox announced the news, then turned around and disappeared. "M&M" didn't know what to do with himself. He looked helpless. He just stood in the middle of the work hall scanning our faces for any reaction, but we were stunned too.

"Congrats! Now, what is the order for today?" I asked, because standing motionless in the cold hall was the worst freezing experience I have ever had.

"I know as much as we all know since this morning, and nothing has been added so far. I will check work docs and get back to you, but you all know what to do, anyway. So, let's go back to work," said "M&M," once he could speak again. He was relieved that we didn't boo him out. He was right, we knew what to do. "M&M" also knew that we needed him on the line to keep production at speed. He checked orders, told us what needed to be done then returned on the line like nothing changed.

After lunch, we went for a smoke together as usual.

"Can you tell me what happened to our 'previous supervisor'?" I asked. Curiosity was eating me alive.

"Sure! I don't know!" "M&M" exclaimed, and his face was telling me that he was honest. "The Fox offered me that position and I accepted. He didn't say why our supervisor left and I didn't ask. I was as surprised as you were down in the canteen," "M&M" continued while puffing away his cigarette.

"Well, I hope you know what you signed up for," I said with a smile.

"Yeah, dealing with you will be the hardest challenge," "M&M" smiled back. "Back to work my slave. Orders are waiting!" "M&M" laughed and pretended to whip me.

The Christmas order came, and we were packing gammons only, between two and three thousand kilograms extra after each regular shift. However, for me as main and only packer, it was times four! In the process of packing each gammon, I had to lift and transfer it four times, six days a week. Yeah! Tonnes and tonnes of pork had to be lifted, shifted, and ran with to the delivery section. All that for flat pay rate, no overtime rate; that was only for some people - like the supervisor for example. "M&M" worked with us side by side and tried to keep our team in good spirits. Although long working hours in a noisy environment with physical exhaustion were pushing us to the edge of mental breakdown. We desperately needed something to lift our moods.

Our team was made of many individuals from different parts of both islands and the world. In that configuration, we had a full rainbow of accents from London to Belfast. Some African accents and Polish/Czechs accents on top of that. The Irish accent itself makes the English language sound stronger, harsh, as it swallows some sounds if spoken fast. It all depends on what part of Ireland one comes from. While London accent goes with a specific rhythm, almost phlegmatic, but keeps the melody of speech. It is like comparing the sound of sandpaper on a wooden board with gentle strokes of cotton wool on the baby's face. Not the same sound at all.

Then comes the Belfast accent, which is not even between those two already compared. The English language performed by a person born and raised in Belfast sounds like someone arrhythmically squeezing a "squeaky ball". The speech has a double pace of CPR compressions on a person's chest. I mean no offence to any above, it's simply my own perception of sounds. I was surrounded by them sometimes, and they were hurting my ears as I was learning the language. I wasn't alone in that matter. I checked later and many non-English speakers had similar perceptions about various accents of the English language.

Back at the scene, the bacon production floor. We were all tired of a long working day in a noisy place. Machines were running, radio was blasting, we could hardly hear our thoughts. We all wished to complete the last order as fast as possible.

One of our drivers was born and raised in London where he spent at least fifty years of his life. He wanted to help us with packing, for that he needed small, black bags to pack one batch. He came to "M&M," who had a strong Belfast-like accent to ask where he can find them.

"I am looking for small, black bags. Do you know where those are?" the driver asked for the first time.

"What?" "M&M" replied.

So, the driver went louder with the same question and "M&M" was giving him the same reply, only louder. They couldn't understand each other at all, not a word. They went back and forth a few times already when I came to "M&M"'s table.

"What is it?" I asked the driver because I saw frustration on his face and "M&M"'s face was blank. The driver explained to me what he needed. I went on the other side of the table, closer to "M&M" and asked the same question.

"Oh, that! Go upstairs to the packing room. There is a box of them next to the door." "M&M" shouted directly to the driver.

"What?" The driver shouted back. "M&M" shouted instructions again, and the driver replied to him the same way. *"Gosh! Here we go again,"* I thought, and I moved to the driver's side to pass "M&M"'s instructions. At this particular moment when the driver was giving a thumbs up to "M&M," as a "thank you" gesture I was lost in LMAO, squatting under the table. Both of them watched me for some time, totally not aware what I was laughing about and not sure how to react. I stopped eventually, stood up and waved at them to get closer to me. They were confused but curious, and moved closer.

"You both speak English, it is your mother tongue, and you need me, Polish, to translate English into English! What would you do without me?" I slowly explained the source of my joy and I burst into loud laughter again.

For a few seconds, both of them couldn't comprehend my words because of my strong accent. Once they got my message, they joined me in a massive laugh. We were all in stitches for the rest of that shift.

After that, we had many laughs caused by harsh and melodic accents. These were also helping us during long working hours. With time, my ears adjusted to the Irish accent, but sometimes "M&M" pushed my understanding to its limits.

One day he asked me and The Hawk to clean the chill.

"Please give the room a deep clean. Use the hot water, then spray with soap, brush it, and rinse twice." "M&M" explained slowly.

"Soup?" I asked. The Hawk just looked at "M&M" completely puzzled.

"Soup? What soup?" It was "M&M"'s turn to be confused. "I said soap."

"Nah, you said soup," I insisted. The Hawk nodded his head; he heard the same word.

"Is he crazy? He wants to clean a room with soup?" The Hawk asked me in Czech.

"Oh, come on! SOAP!" "M&M" shouted with frustration.

"Come on, you said soup!" I said again, and I made a gesture of moving a spoon into mouth because "M&M" was already pale and ready to explode. My gesture helped and "M&M" clicked.

"SOAP!" "M&M" said, and he made a gesture of washing hands. I got it instantly, and I went down to my knees with my

LMFAO. The Hawk was still confused. "M&M" repeated the washing hands gesture with a big grin on his face. "SOAP!" "M&M" said softly and laughed. Finally, The Hawk clicked, he padded his forehead with an open palm, like pushing information inside his head. The Hawk laughed.

"Pshonka! We are fucked up with his English!" The Hawk said in Czech again.

"I don't think it's his English, it's his accent and our ears," I said in English, so "M&M" could understand too. Polish and Czech languages were to our advantage, but it wasn't fair for ignore "M&M" like that. We could've said anything about anyone while the English speaker wouldn't understand. Many English speakers complained about it for years later and I understood that from the day I moved onto the island. I wanted to remain fair to anyone in my presence. If there was anyone who didn't speak our language, I was using English all the time. That rule remains till today.

Here, in this small company, we worked really hard. We worked side by side, we suffered the physical labour equally. There was no space for any form of unfairness towards anyone over there. We were lamenting about long hours to each other. That was bad enough. So, one more complaint about the language barrier would be just one too many.

"No complaints, woman! Just do the job and you will be fine." I was encouraging myself, but my body was aching. I was wrecked after each shift. *"Be grateful that you have a job!"* I was clenching my teeth and crying under the shower. *"How much longer can I manage?"* I was asking myself when that slavery will end, but no one could give me an answer. Actually, there was one person to answer that – me!

I could stop it at any time and point, but I didn't see it! My lack of both confidence and self-trust as well as the illegal situation were holding me back. I knew that I needed another six, maybe seven months to revoke my legal status. The Fox knew it too.

I was lucky to have a job, exhausting and poorly paid, but still better than nothing. I had my passport and I knew I could call in sick for a day or two without being paid sick pay. Shopping, watching movies with The Hawk and Sloth was something I called my mini freedom. On Sundays, we played snooker in the local club, also part of mini freedom. I had my friends and a roof over my head. I was still sharing the bed with The Hawk, though he complained more and more about my snoring. Well, I was tired like a horse after Grand National racing, so I snored. The Hawk knew that too. One Saturday afternoon he took a picture of me dozing off on the chair in the living room. There were days when I was unable to have a simple conversation or watch a movie because I was too tired. I was falling asleep a few seconds after I sat down.

Thankfully, the season for big orders ended just before Christmas Eve and we all enjoyed time off. Just a few days away from bacon and gammons was the greatest blessing in the entire world. We celebrated Christmas with a few more friends. On New Year's Eve, we managed to rescue one more person from the mushroom team, the Drunk Monkey. That rescue shifted our house arrangements and later our friendship.

. . . .

YOUR DAILY EXERCISES

Action Board to empower your visualization

The most important person is you and your love for yourself. You are you; you are the creator of your life. And only you can make those dreams come true. You are taking ownership of your happiness. Here and Now!

Make a personal action board. It is a visual aid to make your goals more appealing and keep your focus on them. Everything goes on your board. Carefully and mindfully picked pictures from magazines will empower your visualisation exercise. Why don't you find them on the Internet and simply print them out? Those pictures do not have the energy of your desire. You need to feel it when you see them, like "Oh, I love it, it speaks to me, it has that shape, colour. It is exactly how I want it to be!" That's the energy in the picture. Be specific! Remember, the more details you add to your wish the better. You can pick just one or few pictures of your goal or goals. Place your action board somewhere you can see it every day, for most of the day. Do not hide it from others. Let them see your goals. If they laugh at them or you, let them do it. Even better, laugh with them. Just say that you are on the path towards them, and you are happy about it. Whatever the others think about you and your dreams is not your issue.

Make a list of as many potential activities as possible, but chose only those you genuinely enjoy. Be bold, creative and consider new and different activities. Step out of your comfort zone. Dare yourself with safety in mind, of course, to activities that you were always scared to do. It will boost your self-confidence.

Find an opportunity to use your strengths, the things that energise you, more often.

Allow yourself to make mistakes. Stop trying to control everything! Be open and receptive to situations instead. Let things be as they are. You will be a much happier, more balanced, compassionate person.

Reward yourself for completing small tasks (e.g., eat your favourite cake after exercises).

3.2 THE DRUNK MONKEY

The Drunk Monkey was one of the pickers from the mushroom farm. Yes, the one who almost gave me a heart attack with her acrobatic figures on the trolley hanging high on the mushroom shelf. She was in her early thirties. She had a work permit; she spoke Russian, but not too much English. She was tall and toned, with dark hair and pale skin. She didn't use much makeup and her natural appearance made her look even younger.

The Drunk Monkey was a great picker and even greater friend to all of us, a kind and honest person. She was a team player and at the same time she was keen to help anyone if asked nicely. It was difficult to get her angry or to get angry with her even when she was annoying. We all do that sometimes, we annoy one another.

She joined our picker's team in the middle of September. She was accepted by the whole gang almost immediately, for her wicked sense of humour. She didn't party all that much, but once she did, she did it all the way to the end or even further. That day she had showed up on the mushroom farm totally drunk was one of her episodes. That's how she earned her nickname: The Drunk Monkey.

The Drunk Monkey and I, often worked on the same shelf, just on its opposite sides. That was an opportunity for us to have a chat which others could not hear. We had some things in common, like broken hearts by ex-partners, dreams about better, brighter futures and our passionate "hate" for mushrooms. We shared our thoughts, our fears, our secrets, and our dreams. She told me her story; I told her mine. We had some things in common, like heart broken by ex-partner, dreams about better, brighter future and our passionate "hate" for mushrooms.

She had her own way of dealing with that "hate" for mushrooms. "My little mushrooms, come to me. I love you all so much. Come to mama, give me more money!" She was saying while she was picking them. Of course, she was saying that in Russian.

Those sarcastic remarks were her way of coping with long days, facing the most hated things in her current situation.

We helped one another with moving and/or swapping trolleys, that fuelled our passionate "hate" for trolleys too.

The differences between us were crucial, but never caused any jealousy. I was illegal; she had papers. I could speak some English; she spoke almost none.

The Drunk Monkey knew The Hawk and Sloth and our relationships. By the way, she was the only one within the pickers who did not believe in the "love story" between me and The Hawk. Although, she had fun watching others fall for that cheap romance produced by us.

She was truly sad when she heard from me that The Hawk and Sloth moved to The Big Town. She was also worried about me, knowing that I am illegal, and for that reason I might be gone one day too. Well, I didn't share everything with her, so she didn't know about my plans with The Hawk and Sloth. It turned out later that she didn't share all her plans with me either.

With the change on the mushroom farm, we were both sent in different directions. She went to another farm that belonged to our boss' brother. She hated it there even more, not because of mushrooms but because the group of pickers who worked there have already established an inner hierarchy. They simply didn't like newcomers. She was fighting for a position, acceptance in a new team. After some time and attempts, she had enough. She had some friends in Belfast and she called them for help.

Belfast was an entirely new experience for her and the most difficult. She was trying hard to learn English fast, but it didn't work. A friend got her a job as a housekeeper in a hotel in Belfast. The accommodation came with the job. She tried her best to keep that job despite lack of language skills. She was doing well, but that language barrier brought her to some misunderstandings with her manager. Her friend acted as an interpreter sometimes, but the person couldn't be there for her all the time, just to help with communication. The manager had enough of lack of communication and The Drunk Monkey lost her job. Automatically, she lost her accommodation, too.

On New Year's Eve morning she called me, crying over the phone.

"I need help, please!" she cried in Russian.

"What's going on?" I asked, also in Russian. Listening to her voice was enough for me to know that she was in some trouble. She never cried in my presence before.

"I've lost my job in Belfast. I was working in a hotel, you know, housekeeper, cleaner. And my manager wasn't satisfied with me because I don't speak English!" she said and burst out crying. She tried to say something more, but her words didn't make sense because she was sobbing.

"Here, I cannot make out a single word what you are saying, girl! Stop crying, please!" I asked her.

She didn't stop, but she tried to explain between sobbing that she got sacked, lost her accommodation too and she must move out today. She said that her friend wasn't willing to help her any more, and she didn't know anybody else who could help her here and now.

"Girl, hold on, let me talk to The Hawk. I will call you back in a few minutes. I promise!" I said. I felt for her, and I was determined to help her. Although, I couldn't do it alone and I couldn't make that decision without first talking to the Czechs.

I woke The Hawk up and told him about the call from The Drunk Monkey. The Hawk wasn't happy about getting up on his day off, but he was worried about our friend.

"Pshonka, what do you want me to do?" The Hawk asked seriously.

"I don't know. Can we help her?" I asked calmly, but my voice was trembling.

"We need to speak to Sloth, too. I need coffee, now!" The Hawk said while moving out of bed.

I flew downstairs and put a kettle on. Sloth was up already and came into the kitchen. He had an instinct of a hunting dog. He knew that something was going on. I told him about the trouble The Drunk Monkey was in.

"That's too bad!" Sloth said, but he didn't offer any solution. Sloth was slow as usual.

The Hawk joined us in the living room, grabbed his cup of coffee and focused on it. I knew he was thinking hard about an action plan to rescue The Drunk Monkey. Me and Sloth were sitting in silence too, waiting patiently for The Hawk's verdict.

"OK, here is what we can do. I have never been to Belfast before, and I don't know the city at all." The Hawk started revealing his thoughts. "That's not a big problem." He said slowly.

"What is the problem then?" I asked. It was hard for me to sit quietly.

"Pshonka, wait! I am thinking." The Hawk lost patience with me. I zipped my mouth, but inside I was boiling. I was thinking about The Drunk Monkey sitting there alone and waiting for a call from me. I knew that feeling. I was there once before too so I could relate.

"Here, how are we going to manage here?" The Hawk continued his thinking process out loud. "Is she going to stay in the little room? How long is she going to stay for?" The Hawk was deep in his thoughts.

"We can decide on that later because she has to move out of the hotel immediately," I reminded The Hawk.

"I know that!" The Hawk wasn't in good form. None of us were. Maybe Sloth was, but he was slow to show it.

"I think that the best option is to go to Belfast as soon as possible to get he out of there. Especially that it is New Year's Eve!" I got my voice back.

"We will have a few days to figure out what to do next," I added less confident.

The Hawk gave me a "killer" look. It simply meant that if I am not going to stop talking, he was going to force me to shut up. I knew that he would come up with something similar, but I was the first to say it out loud. The Hawk didn't like competition in that matter. There was a pregnant moment of silence. Sloth watched both of us. He was counting on a fight between us. Nothing like that happened and Sloth lost interest.

"OK, you two go to Belfast. I will cook," Sloth decided. That unfroze me and The Hawk. I called The Drunk Monkey and asked her about her address in Belfast.

"I don't know the address here! I don't know Belfast!" She yelled into her phone.

"How are we going to find her over there if she doesn't know the address?" This questions was running through my head.

"OK, girl, give me the name of the hotel," I asked. Thankfully, she knew that.

"I don't know the hotel's name, it is close to another hotel but I don't know the other hotel's name either. The other hotel is on a main street in the centre and there is a big TV on the wall next to it. You can see the TV from far away. I will wait at the big TV." That was her description of the place.

"Nice. In the big city, we will look for the big TV." I laughed because it sounded unreal.

"Yes, that's it," she confirmed. She was calmer and happier when I told her that The Hawk and I were coming to rescue her.

"See you soon, girl." I hung up. I went to The Hawk with news about the "Big TV" in the middle of Belfast. The Hawk looked at me like I had three heads.

"Are you for real?" The Hawk asked in disbelief. "I thought that she would give us a proper address!" Now he was disappointed.

"Nothing like that. She has no clue where she is! She only knows there is the big TV hanging on the wall beside the next door hotel, but she doesn't know the name of that hotel." I explained. "What a fricking riddle, don't you think?" I asked myself.

"Gosh, that will be a fricking adventure!" The Hawk yelled. He got excited and stressed at the same time.

Back then, GPS was still a luxury unavailable to us. We were using paper maps, only with roads on them. Some major points were marked on those maps but no big TV, for example. The internet and Google maps were still at a very early stage, although a person with good orientation skills could manage to find the right location. I was nominated a navigator for the trip to Belfast.

We went to a local internet café in the city. Using Google maps I found a few hotels in the city. I opted for a list of directions rather than a map to print out. Simply, that option was cheaper. On the way out of The Big Town, The Hawk stopped at the fuel station. Then we were ready for the rescue mission in the capital of Northern Ireland, Belfast.

Personally, I didn't know much about Northern Ireland. I only knew that it was a part of the United Kingdom. The Hawk knew a bit of history of NI, but he was fully focused on the road and refused to talk to me. While we were travelling up to the North, I noticed changes in the road markings. Then, road signs showed speed in miles, not kilometres.

"What is that about? Miles? Not kilometres?" I had to ask.

"Yeah, English way." The Hawk made his answer as short as possible. He didn't engage in conversation, just kept driving.

The Hawk relaxed a little after an hour of driving, but still wasn't keen to talk. He was deep in his thoughts, planning further decisions related to The Drunk Monkey and all of us.

I was watching the road and absorbed surroundings with my photographic memory. There was a field full of sheep on the left, a field full of caws on the right and the road to Belfast in the middle. Idyllic picture to switch off my mind, just observe and enjoy! My mantra was back: "Everything always works out for me! Everything is well!" I kept repeating it inside my head.

Another half an hour and we were on the outskirts of Belfast. I grabbed the list with printed directions, looking for a signpost to the town centre. We drove along Donegall Road. Semidetached houses looked all the same. Houses of red bricks, clustered together on both sides of the street. They looked dull and depressive in the cold, damp December weather.

We were aiming at Europa Hotel as the key point; we turned left into Sandy Row. A massive colourful graffiti appeared in front of our eyes. Well, I was mesmerised by those pictures on the side of the buildings, more than The Hawk, he was so tensed and tried to keep up with my instructions.

"Pshonka!!! Which way now?" The Hawk yelled at me. His voice brought my focus back into the car. I looked at my printed script, then I looked outside.

"Turn right now!" I yelled! The Hawk made an immediate manoeuvre, squeezing in between cars parked on both sides of the street.

"Pshonka! Where are we going?" The Hawk had some doubt in his voice.

"You said I am the navigator so listen to me, keep going!" I ordered. We came to the junction at Shaftesbury Square. Europa Hotel to our left but we could only go in one direction, we had to take left. The moment The Hawk was turning to the left I looked to the right. The big TV was in the opposite direction.

"The Hawk, the big TV is there!" I yelled into his ear and pointing to the right. The Hawk jumped and almost caused a collision with another car.

"F*&&%^, you scared the crap out of me!" The Hawk yelled back at me in terror. He was moving his head to the left and right like a puppet. "I can't turn right here!" The Hawk pointed to the road sign. The driver in the car behind us hit the horn impatiently.

"Go to the left, then take the first right," I instructed him, scanning through my prints. The Hawk drove down the road slowly, keeping to the right side of the road in case he would miss the right turn.

"*Here, right!*" I yelled again. This time The Hawk didn't jump, just gave me his "killer" look. Again we squeezed through a narrow street until we got to another junction.

"Turn right here," I said calmly, trying not to annoy him anymore. "Straight, keep going," I said with relief. I could see the damn big TV in front of us. "Here we are," I said with a big grin on my face. The Hawk didn't smile at all. He was busy looking at the road, highly concentrated on following my directions. We passed the hotel and parked in the first available space. I called The Drunk Monkey.

"Hi girl, we are here, next to the big TV," I told her in Russian.

"I am coming now!" she said eagerly and hung up. I looked at The Hawk. He was catching his breath and trying to relax.

"We did it! You are a great driver!" I praised him to cheer him up. The city was a massive challenge for him, and I knew it. I would have done it myself if I could, but the risk that the police would stop us was very high, and that would cause far more trouble, for both of us.

"Yeah, right. We almost hit another car," The Hawk said slowly. He knew his abilities, too. He was calming down and got out of the car for a cigarette. "Where is she?" The Hawk asked.

Then The Drunk Monkey appeared. She was carrying a few plastic bags; she was trying to wave at us and run across the road towards us at the same time. She looked like a huge plastic tornado rolling across the road. She dropped her bags on the ground next to the car and gave us both big hugs and kisses on both cheeks. She was as happy as a monkey with a banana.

"I have two more suitcases to take from the cafe over there. Can you help me, please?" she asked The Hawk politely. The Hawk was already on the move to help her.

I noticed that The Hawk not only cooled down but also softened his face with a gentle smile. Just for a split second a spark appeared in his eyes. "Hold on! Do I see what I see?" A reflection regarding that scene appeared in my mind. The Drunk Monkey was happy to see us both. She didn't flirt, she was grateful that we were rescuing her. Although The Hawk lightened up the moment he saw her coming. All the stress related to driving to and through a big city just disappeared. *"Oh, I'll be damned, he has some feelings for her! Oh, she has a secret admirer, and she is not aware of that... or maybe she knows? Hmm...? We shall see."* I thought to myself as I was watching the two of them walking back with her suitcases.

Once all was packed, The Hawk was ready to drive again. I took the front seat because he still needed directions.

"Go straight ahead, then take the right at the fork, then go straight again," I told him. He just nodded his head without any comments. *"Ooh, that's something new. Usually, he would ask twice to check with me if I was absolutely sure.*" I made a mental note of The Hawk's strange behaviour, and I turned to The Drunk Monkey.

"How did you end up here?" I asked The Drink Money in Russian. Ah, right, The Hawk's Russian was basically limited to a few words. Although, he didn't mind us to use that language. Usually, he was guessing what the conversation was about. If he didn't hear his name in the middle of the chat he keep quiet. Me and The Drunk Monkey could speak freely.

The Drunk Monkey repeated the same story she tried to tell me over the phone, only this time without sobbing. Well, she was almost singing like a rescued bird that was free again. She added a few details and a time frame to her story. She said that she left the other mushroom farm soon after I left ours. She couldn't stand the atmosphere between pickers over there. The pressure, the competition and all that crap.

The Drunk Monkey called her old friend, someone she knew back home. Her friend helped her to get the job in the hotel. Unfortunately, her friend was not aware that she doesn't speak much English. The manager kept The Drunk Monkey over there because they were short-staffed; Christmas was coming, and the hotel was busy. The friend was constantly bombarded with calls from The Drunk Monkey asking to speak on her behalf. Other calls to her friend were from the manager who constantly complained about lack of communication with The Drunk Monkey.

Altogether, it was too much for her friend who had already left that job and didn't want to take any more calls from either of them. The hotel manager was really pissed off with both of them. Frustration took over, and he sacked The Drunk Monkey on the spot, giving her less than 24 hours to leave. She called me because she didn't have anyone else she could trust.

The Drunk Monkey was entirely grateful for us rescuing her. On the way to The Big Town, she was constantly talking about it. The Hawk wasn't listening, he just focused on the road, but I had to listen to it.

"OK, girl, don't worry, we will figure something out for you. But today is the last day of the year, so let's leave all the bad things in the old year!" I suggested. "Let the best days of the old year become the worst days of the new year," I cited a Jewish proverb. The Drunk Monkey laughed and finally relaxed.

"Are we having a party tonight?" The Drunk Monkey asked.

"We? I don't know about you and the Czechs, but I am out tonight. I am going to see my new friend whom I've met at the internet café. Just a few drinks in the bar." I revealed my plans.

"What about you, The Hawk? Any plans for tonight?" I asked our driver, but he just mumbled something I couldn't hear.

"Nah, he doesn't like to talk while he is driving on the motorway," I explained to The Drunk Monkey. "He needs to stay focused on the road. We will find out later," I added.

We arrived in The Big Town late that afternoon. The Sloth was waiting for us with a lovely meal. During the meal, we had an important conversation about home arrangements. Though The Hawk was deep in his thoughts again at the beginning but later he joined the conversation.

His face was burning with blush and his eyes were shining like he was thinking about something really naughty. *"Would he propose to The Drunk Monkey to share a bed with him the same way as with me?"* I thought while I was watching The Hawk. He was glowing. *"Nah, he is too shy to do it straight away,"* I thought, and he proved me wrong.

"Pshonka, would you be so kind and move to the little bedroom downstairs?" The Hawk asked with no hesitation. My jaw simply dropped. *"He is kicking me out of the bed!"* I thought in panic before I answered. *"Why should I stay there, anyway? There is nothing going to happen between us. So?"* My second and third thought.

"Actually, I was about to propose that," I said with confidence. The three of them were looking at me like I had three heads. I saw different emotions on each of the faces. The Hawk's face expressed admiration that I got his intentions without explanation. Our transcendental connection was confirmed.

Sloth was shocked. Possibly, because he still remembered my initial reaction to that bedroom. Maybe he thought that there was something going on between me and The Hawk, despite our declarations of pure friendship.

The Drunk Monkey's gratitude was written all over her face. She did not suspect The Hawk's intentions then or what was to happen between them soon. It took them some time though.

For me, it was a signal to move on. The Universe was kicking my butt to challenge me again. Well, six weeks was enough for recovery. In my opinion it wasn't, I didn't feel strong enough to try something new and possibly on my own. I counted my blessings, although, secretly I was still crying for help. At the same time, I was begging for relief and asking for changes.

"Would that discomfort of staying in that small, dark, cold bedroom kick me up, down, or out? Or in any other direction?" I asked myself after making my proposal. *"It depends on what you want, and which way you want to go!"* My inner being answered.

"What?" I asked all of them. "You didn't know that I have a big heart?" I laughed. None of them were able to answer or didn't know what to say to that. The Drunk Monkey and The Hawk jumped to their feet and started to move things up and down. Sloth just shook his head and followed them. I prepared my old-new bedroom.

It took us twenty minutes to reorganise our house, we were ready to celebrate the upcoming New Year! A new trio went shopping, and I was getting ready for a night out. I was hoping for some fun, a good party where I meet new people and learn more about my new friend.

Then, I got a text message from my new friend that he was running late. He might be in The Big Town before ten that night. *"Oh, are you for real?"* I was thinking and feeling stood up. *"I've done a good deed today why can't I have my reward?"* I was disappointed. *"Go and have fun. Meet other people! You deserve it!"* I encouraged myself. I sent a text back, just to meet me at the pub whenever he arrives and I went there on my own.

In the pub I saw a few faces I had seen before in the internet café. I had a couple of casual chats with some of them. They had already made plans to go to some private parties later that night. No invitation for me though. *"Fine, I am a stranger to all of you and vice versa.*" My loneliness has just hit me, but I was keeping a straight face. "*I need somebody, someone for me,*" I thought.

My new friend appeared at half past ten. The pub was closing at half past eleven because the staff also wanted to celebrate the New Year. For an hour, I was listening to the long list of complaints and excuses that made me sick, but I was sober. I really regretted not drinking more before he came. At least I would have an excuse to be sick and to end that sort of ridiculous date.

"*A fricking Happy New Year to me!*" I thought when I finally said good night to my new friend and walked home on my own. Almost like Cinderella I left my not-so-much Prince Charming before midnight. I almost lost my shoe running away from him as fast as possible and to get home on time to celebrate a New Year with people I knew and appreciated. My new friend did not think I was his Cinderella, he never tried to contact me afterwards. "*Well, maybe I dodged a bullet? Or it wasn't meant to be?*" I thought, still a bit disappointed.

I welcomed a New Year with my favourites, two funny Czechs and The Drunk Monkey. We were a new pack, and we wished one another all the best in a New Year. That night we had a few drinks, funny dances, and loads of laughter.

From what you have read so far, would you guess what I wished for? Exactly! I wished for freedom, change of life from slavery to freedom of movement and choice of life. I wished that new, great love would find me and care for me, that it would bring, joy, health, wealth, and happiness. All the great things for me in this New Year!

For all of that, I already felt grateful and more beautiful things were on the way. I was also grateful for the past year. For friendships, the helpful and those unhelpful. For events, people, and places I'd been. I was grateful for everything.

It was a big lesson for me, a massive experience, only I didn't know then how lucky I was to have all of that. I was physically and mentally exhausted. Was it worth this high price I was paying? Yes, it was, however the biggest realisation came many years later.

Then, during all that time I had the most precious thing not available to many slaves all over the world. I had my freedom! Freedom of choice and the decision was entirely mine, minus circumstances. Though, no matter what circumstances I was in, I was still holding my passport and I could leave immediately. I totally rejected that thought.

I had a new job, and I moved to a place where I had more prospects. I was making a bit more money, and I had friends. Hooray and yay! I got what I asking for.

Really? Was there anything else? Or was that it? Hold on a moment. Did I ask for unbearably hard, physical work? Did I ask for a cold, damp room? Did I ask for sharing a bed with a friend who was not attracted to me and vice versa? Oh, no I didn't! Or did I? When?

Moreover, where are those opportunities offered by living in the city? Where are my chances of developing my language and skills? Where are all those new people I should meet and make connections with, those new friendships? Where are my big dreams about a bright and successful career? Where is my new, true love? NO, No and no, I didn't ask those questions, so why was I disappointed?

"Yeah, woman, you got what you asked for! No refund here." My inner being was laughing at me. I was missing the precision, specification, and detailed description of my dreams. To do it properly, you need to be emotionally connected to your dream to smell it, touch it, hear it, see it, taste it. The most important, feel that you already have it!

Another "AHA" moment, make sure you feel it first, feel every detail, feel it with your heart, soul, and every cell of your body.

Be specific about every single detail. Many years later, someone told me that just asking for an abundance is not the way. You may receive an abundance of diarrhoea instead of an abundance of money, love, and happiness. Be specific!

Sometimes introspection helps to get clarity on what you want. For that you can use Ho'oponopono statements – check Your Daily Exercises.

YOUR DAILY EXERCISES

Helping Yourself first also helps others

It's showing compassion for yourself and others. Of course, if you can and want to help others without expecting anything in return; be honest, if you can do something, say it. If you cannot, say that too. It's not about financial support only. Share what you can share. Sometimes, just give a little bit of your time, just a bit of patience, just listen to another person. It might be a massive support for the person and enormous satisfaction for you.

Introspection with Ho'oponopono statements.

It is a slow process of looking into yourself to unfold the truth about yourself. Ho'oponopono comes from Hawaii. It is a ritual of releasing negativity from your life and energy. It helps to deal with the past, people, past mistakes, behaviours which no longer serve you and you need to release them to move on. Use HO'OPONOPONO four statements, the order doesn't matter:

"I love you..."(say who, what, etc.).

"Please forgive me..."(say to whoever it is related to).

"I am sorry..." (say to whoever it is related to).

"Thank you..." (say what for).

3.3 THE MAGICAL HOLIDAY BACK HOME –
UNFOLDING THE TRUTH

Despite all those beautiful signs of wishes granted, I was exhausted physically and on the edge of emotional break down. For over six months, I was on an emotional swing with anxiety poking my consciousness and fear kicking the back of my head. I needed a holiday, a proper, long, and well-deserved break. Well, for that to happen I had to wait another four months.

Meanwhile, The Fox took full advantage of my situation by pretending and promising an appointment with his solicitor to sort out my papers for a work permit. The appointment with the solicitor happened about three weeks before new members, including Poland, joined the European Union. That act granted freedom of movement for new members of the EU, and employment rights under EU legislation.

The solicitor told me that the entire process of getting a work permit would take longer than three weeks, and after that time I wouldn't need that anyway. He was wrong, but I had no clue about that either.

"So, what is the point?" the solicitor asked. I tried to explain that my holiday would happen before that date and the work permit would allow me to return from the holiday.

"Change your holiday date," the solicitor suggested.

"Well, not so easy and cheap to do," I told him without getting into any details. My flights were already booked. At the end of our meeting, he assured me that he would send my papers to the emigration department anyway. I doubt that ever happened.

Nevertheless, The Fox was happy to issue me a letter of employment for travelling purposes. I wasn't so sure about that, and my intuition was screaming with fear at the back of my mind. *"What if I cannot return here before Poland becomes a full member of the EU?"* I asked myself.

Then I said to myself: *"Everything always works out for me."* Although I was not so sure about it. Without a proper and convincing answer, equipped only with The Fox's letter, I went home for the first time in ten months.

A week at home did its magic. I recharged physically and mentally, surrounded by familiar faces and places. It felt like I was away for ten years, not ten months. So many things changed at home too, a few of them were so completely new to me that it made me feel uncomfortable. Why? What was it? I couldn't put my finger on it.

On the day before my return to Ireland, I was having a pint of lager with the guys from my neighbourhood. Before I left the country we had drinks and played pool often. They were asking me where I was working and how much I was getting per hour. Two simple answers: bacon and the rate per hour satisfied them completely. Neither of them was interested in how hard it was to do that job and how I felt about it. Although all of them knew how to calculate Euro into Polish currency.

Someone said: "So, you are leaving tomorrow, right?" I just nodded. "You are going there to make more money and come back here loaded, right?" The person continued before I had a chance to respond, "I know a few people working there already. They are making tons of money, but they forgot their old friends here," he spat out with venom of accusation in his voice. That was too much for me. *"if only you knew how hard it is,"* I thought, but I didn't bother to explain my reality and I changed a subject.

"Good for them! I will need more alco than money to erase my memories. Last round is on me," I announced and went to the bar to order the last round for that night. While I was waiting for that order, it hit me why I felt that something wasn't right there.

My perception shifted drastically! I was sitting there with some people who couldn't offer me anything but jealousy for me making relatively more money than they did. None of them even asked: "Are you OK with what you are doing there? How do you feel about migration? Are you homesick?" Even before I left for the first time, they couldn't help me with anything. And now, the only thing that was bothering them was the comparison of our incomes. They perceived and looked at me in the old, communistic Polish way: "You live abroad, in the West, so you must be wealthy. You are better off than we are here." All about money and status.

I wanted life, love, and laughter. I took a risk to get it, to find my purpose and a life without fear. Instead, it hit me even stronger to realise that I was living on the edge of fear constantly for the past ten months. They never knew what I really wanted. There was no point in explaining it to them.

I got the last round of drinks for my companions. I couldn't call them friends any more. They were just people I knew in my previous life, which ended on the day I left my country. So, there were not long goodbyes, just "sayonara" which means "I don't know when I will see you again."

I left the pub and walked home on my own. I felt a little of bitterness mixed with sadness that some of the people I knew most of my life had such shallow view on life. We had some good laughs and good times, no doubt. The difference was that I moved on to seek more good times and more laughs. They could've done the same, but they didn't, their choice. Were they too scared to do the same? Possibly.

Not that I was a hero, but it was more about feeling the fear and doing it anyway. Curiosity, temptation to be in a new situation, radical changes, and challenges. That shifted my perception of life, the way I see people, and my purpose here and now. *"Let them be. You are here to do something different than that. I went through some crap; I can do anything, and fear cannot stop me anymore,"* I thought to myself.

· ·

Leave the past in the past, forgive yourself and move on. Forgive others. Whatever they are doing in their life and with their life is not your business. Those are their choices. Let them be!

Make your mistakes. Those are your lessons to learn so that you can make things different next time. Pay attention to all those lessons. They are disclosing your weaknesses and your emotions associated with them. Make a list of all the improvements you need to make, put them on your action board. For every weak point, propose at least three ways to improve it.

Once you complete them, make an honest inventory list and you will surprise yourself with how many things you can turn from disaster to success. You will raise like a Phoenix from the ashes! Focus on new approaches to your projects.

Trust your intuition. Believe in yourself, love yourself, and be kind to yourself. You've got everything you need and be grateful for it. You are not only going to survive, but you will also thrive!

3.4 THE UNFORGETTABLE RETURN TO THE ISLAND

Early morning the next day, I went to Berlin airport to get my first flight, to London Stansted where I had a connecting flight to Dublin. I held tightly to my safe-conduct pass issued by The Fox. I put whole my faith in that letter. It was a document confirming that I could return to Ireland without trouble and lies.

I still remembered my first entrance "act" at Dublin airport almost a year earlier. I had to make up a story about the wrong date on my return ticket. I made it believable. But that was a one off for me. I was taught to be honest and speak the truth because it is easier to remember than the lies. I was convinced that I could be honest and speak the truth having this letter with me.

Also, the upcoming inauguration of the new EU members, including Poland, was to my advantage. It was, in my opinion and deepest belief, that no one would even think about stopping me from entering Dublin just a week before that historical event.

The flight from Berlin to London Stansted was pleasant and on time. I collected my luggage, and I went straight to border control. I was completely focused on my next flight. *"Just get through the emigration check point and off I go..."* I thought and joined the long queue for border control.

All London airports are busy all the time. It wasn't unusual that it was taking a long time to get through border control, so I waited f patiently for forty minutes for my turn to come.

Finally, the officer called me to the stand. With my nicest smile, I approached him and passed my passport over to him.

"Good morning, officer," I smiled. He just looked at me like I just killed his cat.

"Where are you travelling to today, Miss?" *The* officer asked coldly.

"To Dublin," I answered, keeping my smile.

"What is the purpose of your travel to Dublin?" The officer continued while going through my passport.

"I live and work there. In The Big Town to be exact," I said honestly, and I passed the letter from The Fox. The officer just scanned through the letter, then gave me the diabolical look. I could have read his face, like: *"Oh no, Miss I don't think you are going to reach your destination today!"*

"Miss please wait here. I will be back," the officer said with a tiny smirk on the left side of his mouth and went to the back office. My smile disappeared from my face, and I froze there. *"What the hell? Is he for real?"* I thought. *"HELP! Anyone, help?"* My panic mode just switched on. *"Why? What is wrong with the letter?"* My brain was running on and on like a hamster on the running wheel.

About ten minutes later, which felt like ten centuries, the officer came back. This time I was sure his face was saying, "I told you so! You are not going to reach your destination today!"

"Miss I called Dublin border control, and I explained to them that you are travelling there for employment purposes with the letter issued by your employer," the officer started. "The officer at the Irish border control office informed me that you are not allowed to enter Ireland without a proper work permit," he finished with a cold as ice voice.

I was speechless, entirely frozen in brain and body. Not a single thought appeared in my mind for some time. I just looked at the officer like he was an alien. The officer continued his duties without the slightest interest in my state. He had seen that before so many times that he could not be bothered to even pretend that he cares.

"Miss please fallow me to the office," the officer ordered and started walking towards a glass door behind him. I couldn't move at all. The officer looked back and shouted: "Miss this way, please!" I forced my legs to move in his direction. The officer led me to the emigration office, passed my documents to the next officer, and left the office. I stood in the middle of the office completely confused.

"Have a seat, Miss" the next officer said gently, clearly seeing my state. I moved to the nearest chair and dropped my full body weight on it. Gravity helped to drop my luggage with a bang next to me. My senses were coming back. I was slowly coming back to the reality.

"Miss do you need a drink?" the officer asked politely.

"Yes, please," I said quietly and burst into tears because at that moment I realised what was going to happen. *"I am not going to Ireland today!"* It was running through my mind. All my lowest and most negative emotions flowed like water on the millwheel pushing out my tears, now flowing like a waterfall. I couldn't stop crying.

"Miss please calm down," the officer said, clearly losing his patience. "Do you understand your situation?" he asked slowly. I just shook my head. My waterfall of tears continued. I was on the edge of dehydration.

"Do you need an interpreter? What language?" he continued.

"Polish, please," I said through my tears.

"But you understand me, do you?" the officer asked.

"I do... but... not... every... thing..." I answered with pauses between every word when I was catching my breath.

"OK, sit tight. I will call interpreting services and come back to you," the officer said formally, stood up and walked quickly towards the door, like he was worried that he was going to be drowned in my tears.

I don't know how long I was sitting there alone and crying my eyes out. I was drowning in my sorrow accompanied by a physical pain of defeat. "How the hell did that happen?" I thought over and over.

In my thoughts, I cursed The Fox and his letter. I cursed my habit of being honest. I cursed everyone and everything that stood in the way of my return to Ireland. That pill of bitterness was too big to swallow. *"After all I had been through and what I survived, was I not allowed to return to gain something better? WHY NOT?"* I was asking myself and another wave of tears gushed out.

After some time, the officer appeared with a Polish interpreter and the interview began. The officer gave me another glass of water and, without wasting more time started to ask standard questions. I finally calmed down, or maybe I didn't have more tears to cry, or maybe because I felt supported at least in terms of language.

The interpreter was fluent in both languages, Polish and English, and easy to understand. That caught my attention more than what the officer was asking me about.

Through the whole interview, I had just one thought: *"Woman, I want to be fluent in English like you and I want your job!"* That was the wish I "spelled" in the moment of despair. I didn't know then that any wish spelled even in such a negative situation, but highly charged with emotions, would have any power to come true. Now, I know, because it became real a few years later. Also, a few years later, I received the answer to my desperate "WHY" at London Stansted Airport.

I was stopped there for that purpose, to discover my path, to clearly state what I want. The stress and tears weren't for nothing. All of that was there to unlock my highest emotions and to spell my wish. That is why I called this chapter "The unforgettable return to the island". It's hard to forget something horrible and beautiful at the same time.

Of course, I do not wish anyone to go through such stress, anxiety, mental meltdown filled with tears in order to gain the highest level of emotions that would make a powerful wish come true. That happened to me for a reason long before I discovered a much more pleasant and easy way to reach strong emotions. It's called MEDITATION!

Back to the London Stansted Airport where I was waiting for the judgement and punishment. The officer completed the interview and all the paperwork.

"I am going to check flights to Berlin tonight. I will rebook your ticket to Dublin to return to Berlin as soon as possible," the officer informed me and left the office. The interpreter also left for a short break. Shortly, the officer returned with the interpreter to inform me that the next flight to Berlin was in three hours. He also explained the boarding procedures for that flight.

"We are going to hold your passport and ticket. One of our officers will escort you to the plane and pass your documents to the captain to hold them during your flight. You will receive your documents after landing in Berlin." The officer went through the procedures smoothly, so did the interpreter. "Any questions?" the officer asked.

"Yes, where are you going to hold me? And can I use a toilet, please?" I asked as I felt that my spacious bladder was going to burst. I didn't need another disaster that day.

"I will take you down to the secluded waiting room. There is a toilet you can use freely. There are also free of charge machines with sandwiches, drinks, and snacks you can use," the officer said almost proud of the official hospitality.

"Thank you," I said quickly and grabbed my luggage, signalising that I was ready to go. I also said thank you to the interpreter, but she did not respond, just left the room without saying "bye" or even "kiss my rear".

"No problem," the officer responded automatically, then opened the door and led me to the secluded waiting room.

I was alone in the waiting room. I dropped my bags and ran to the toilet. "*Damn, so many tears and still so much fluids to pee with,*" I thought, feeling at least one kind of relief that day.

In any other situation, I would think that I was privileged to have a room with free food, drinks, and snacks to myself. Although, I wasn't in a mood to appreciate it at all. I was too wounded, too devastated to even notice that.

I desperately needed to get help with transport from Berlin to my town in Poland. It wouldn't be that tricky if I had money and credit on my phone. I was analysing the options, in my head.

There were only two alternatives available and neither of them was pleasant even to consider. I would rather prefer to sell my kidney to get money, anything to avoid asking my mother for help. Situation with my aunt in Berlin was similar.

My relationship with both of them was far from good. Both would react in a similar way to any of my failures. It would give them something they could point out on any occasion. Both would spread the news within the closest family with a sick satisfaction.

As the quick organ sale was not available at the time, I had to consider option A. I arrive in Berlin, late in the evening and call my mother asking her to contact her friends in Berlin. They were able to confirm if anyone was driving from Berlin back to Poland that night. Calling my mother also meant asking her for money. I will also have to explain what happened in London. Option B, call my aunt in Berlin and ask for the same favour. Those options felt awful and made me sick, but I didn't have a choice. I went to my mother for help. Second defeat within less than 24 hours. I wasn't sure which one was worse.

Don't get me wrong, I love my mother and she loves me back, but on her own terms that has entirely disagreed with me since I was thirteen years old. We are on the opposite ends of the love stick. Despite some efforts, flexibility and the degree of acceptance, the stick remains stiff.

I had a few hours to prepare myself for the phone call to my mother. I wondered how long I would have to listen to her, *"I told you so…"* as if it would change anything. *"I am an adult, and I am allowed to make my own mistakes."* I prepared my own speech in my head.

Then I realised that I was falling into the dangerous spiral of self-doubt. *"Hold on a moment, I am in enough crap at the moment, and whatever my mother would say doesn't matter. She can't change the past, turn back time. It had already happened! I can change my future. I already am by accepting that I need my mother to help me. I accept that with all consequences and blessings. So, what's next?"* I was reasoning with myself by talking myself out of negative thoughts and emotions. *"Calm down first, think woman!"* Exactly in that order.

I started pacing between vending machines, completely focused on counting my steps to focus on less emotional tasks. Slowly, I was getting calmer with every step. When I got tired of walking, I stood in front of one of the vending machines and I was counting items in the machine. From the top shelf to the bottom and up again. It was strange. I had never done anything like that, but it felt surprisingly soothing. I don't know how long it took me to finally "switch" from negative thoughts and emotions, but it worked!

When I felt mentally "unlocked", opened and ready to think about my options, I got into a full conversation with my inner being, the wiser one.

"Answer here and now: do you want to go back to Ireland?" My inner being asked.

"Of course, I want to go back to Ireland. What kind of question is that?" I was almost insulted by that question.

"Sheesh you! Cry me a river, babe! I do not argue, I am asking! I am trying to help, so listen!" My inner being is always straight and fair with me. *"Think, what do you need to do once you get back to your mummy?"* My inner being also knows my relationship with my mother.

"Come on, there is no time and space for your sarcastic comments. Well, I will contact 'Skinny'. She is the only person I know that always has money. She doesn't like to lend any money to any of her friends. She is afraid that she might lose a friend because of money. But she will understand an emergency and I never borrowed money from her. Alright, money sorted!" I reached my first point of the magnificent rescue plan.

"What next, sweetie?" My inner being softened its voice.

"I will need to wait until the 2nd of May when, Poland becomes an official member of EU. Any date after that, will be a safe date to fly back to Ireland. Flight date sorted. I will need internet access. Damn, 'Skinny' again. I will buy her a bottle of Ballantine for all the help." I got my second point of the rescue plan.

"What else, honey?" My inner being was getting really sweet with me.

"Oh, yes! I need to contact The Hawk and let him know what happened. The Hawk will pass it onto The Fox." I stated the next point of my plan.

"Hm, by the way. Do you want to stay and still work for The Fox?" My inner being asked.

"Hell, no! Have you lost your mind?" I went on with my inner being, well technically with myself.

"Hold on! Who is losing her mind?" I slowed down that inner conversation.

"Alright, so what do you need to do?" My inner being completely ignored my confusion.

"I need to stay at bacon factory for a while and get an appointment to register myself in a job office to get an insurance number that will help me find another job! Yes! That's the plan!" I was proud of myself.

I was so engrossed in my thoughts, still standing at the vending machine, talking to it like 'a mad person' that I didn't see the security officer enter the waiting room.

He has been there for some time and enjoyed the show. His amusement was all over his face when he cleared his throat to get my attention. I jumped on the spot and looked at him like he was my worst enemy. I almost shouted "What?" because I was torn out of my precious "zone" of completing and contemplating my plan.

"Excuse me, I didn't mean to scare you." He saw my surprise. Still, he was unable to hide his big smile from the entertainment he just watched.

I was just staring at him, mute and motionless. *"Oh, yeah? You didn't mean it! Of course, not. You had fun watching me here!"* I thought while my senses were returning to me.

"It's time to go," the officer said calmly. Finally, he noticed the lack of my reaction and his smile disappeared.

"Yes! Of course, time to go!" I exclaimed, and I thought it was definitely time for my fun. "Time to go where?" I asked gently, still gawking at him with the most innocent face I could bring out.

"Ehm, you know, boarding... your flight to Berlin." He waved at me with an envelope in his hand. The officer was confused, evidently not sure if I had already "lost my marbles" because he just witnessed my deep conversation with the vending machine. Come on, have you seen a mentally stable person talking to a vending machine? The officer's face said more than he intended. I couldn't help myself and I burst into loud laughter.

"Ah, that!" I said. "OK, let's go!" I was laughing and picking up my bags. The officer's next facial expression was, *"I give up."* Possibly he has never experienced a person in a good mood during the deportation process. More than possible! Deportation is not a funny business at all. My happiness had nothing to do with my deportation, but he didn't know that. My intuition sent me a vibration that the officer just judged my unusual behaviour in the category "she is crazy, stay alert!". I couldn't pass that moment without having my amusement by watching him being even more confused by my happiness.

The officer was almost racing to the gate through the back corridors. Luckily, I was able to keep with his pace due to my "bacon-fitness". Once we reached the gate, he asked me to stand right behind him while he was talking to the airline's ground staff.

The boarding hasn't started yet, but all passengers were in line already. Passengers at the front were close, but they couldn't hear what the officer was saying. They were staring at me full of mixed feelings from curiosity to admiration. It was evident, they looked at me expressing something between "Who are you?" and "How dare you be in front of us?" I absorbed the atmosphere and thought: *"No hard feelings, but you will never know!"*

"Please do not start boarding other passengers before I come back from the plane," the officer instructed the ground staff.

"I have the VIP treatment, for once!" I thought to myself, it felt good. I was standing there with a charming smile and feeling that "everything always works out for me". Brilliant!

The officer waved at me with that envelope again, pointing towards the gate door. We went down the stairs, then walked across the tarmac ground and climbed the front door stairs of my plane. The officer asked a stewardess to call the captain out. The man appeared at the door. That was some captain, handsome, mid-forties, German. There was something polite about him. The security officer was pointing the envelope at me while he was explaining who I was and what to do with me. He was staring at me while listening to the security officer. The captain just nodded to the security man when he passed him the envelope. Then the security guy turned to me.

"Bye!" he shouted to me like I was deaf and disappeared into thin air. He didn't wait for my response. I just waved goodbye and smiled to the air.

After that the captain pointed the envelope at me and gave instructions to his staff. Next, he turned to me and waved the envelope.

"I got you!" The captain waved the envelope with my passport in it. "I will give it that back to you in Berlin," he said to me with a kind smile and went back into the cockpit, taking the envelope with him. The head steward showed me the seat in the front row. All three seats for me!

A few minutes later, the rest of the passengers appeared on board. Some of them gave me a serious look of jealousy. Possibly, they bought priority access, but I managed to beat to it. I am the one person with the VIP treatment, enjoying the VIP seat at the front! Special person with a big smile on her face!

Seriously, I couldn't care less what they thought and felt watching me in front of them. *"If only you knew what I went through today... and what I am going to face soon after landing in Berlin, you wouldn't swap places with me. Trust me!"* I thought while grinning at those who were giving me the judgemental look. I could sense their negative vibrations so strongly that it made me feel even stronger and more confident about how to execute my plan.

The crew manager announced that all passengers are on board.

"I will be back; I am going to Ireland next week!" I thought at the same moment the stewardess closed the plane door. I got the shivers, it felt powerful! *"When one door closes, another door opens!"*[9] I recalled the quote and reminded myself that I need to follow my plan immediately. Step one, right after landing.

---

9 "When one door closes, another opens; but we often look so long and so regretfully upon the closed door that we do not see the one which has opened for us." – Alexander Graham Bell.

"*Relax, everything will be fine. Follow your plan, woman!*" I was reassuring myself to trust the Universe.

Despite my positive thoughts and belief, the Universe did not spare me surprises! Any contrasting events? Check! Just to check if my inner being and I still have the connection. I felt like WE – me and my inner being – both failed epically. We did not pay enough attention to details while creating the first rescue plan at Stansted Airport.

"*We?*" My annoying inner being protested. "*Mon amour! My role is to tell you that there are other ways, options to achieve your goals and feel good about them all on the path towards them. Your role is to work on details, be specific with them!*"

"*Oh, YOU! Watch me! I can do it!*" I replied to myself. Again! Insane, ha? Not really.

Positive self-talking saved my sanity so many times that I've lost count. Still it is the best habit I have ever acquired.

How many baby steps did I need to get back to Ireland? You will find out in my next book. See you soon!

· ·

Just to clarify, meditation is not for monks only! It is for everyone. With simple instructions and personal time contribution, anyone can learn how to quieten their mind.

Some claim that seventeen seconds is enough time to reach the highest level of emotions. Yes, it's possible with some practice. However, I respect individuality and I personally believe that "one size doesn't fit all".

Everyone who wants to experience meditation needs to find their own timing, that can only be discovered through trying. Start with small steps. Give yourself 1 minute for a few days. Then try 5 minutes and add another 5 minutes whenever you feel ready. And another 5 minutes, up to a total of 20 minutes just for yourself. You do not need more than 20 minutes a day, but the difference is immense. I highly recommend giving it a try, today, even now!

In Your Daily Exercises, you will find an introduction to meditation.

YOUR DAILY EXERCISES

Introduction to Meditation

Meditation is not for monks only! It is for everyone. Anyone can learn how to quieten their mind, using simple instructions and contributing your personal. So, take it easy, take small steps. Meditation an easy way to calm Your mind in small steps.

Start with 1 minute. Sit upright, comfortable, relax your body. Take slow, deep breaths in and out. And again. Feel that all the tension in your body is relieved. Breathe normally, close your eyes and start counting backwards from 60 to 1.

Focus on numbers, try to imagine all subsequent numbers in your mind. Thoughts will appear between those numbers; no worries, just observe them passing and bring your focus to following numbers.

When you reach number 1, before you open your eyes, just say thank you to yourself for that 1 minute. Open your eyes. Observe your feelings, emotions, thoughts.

Try it again during your day, on your break at work, on the toilet (yes, perfect spot for 1 minute of relaxation), on the train, bus. DO NOT TRY IT WHILE YOU ARE DRIVING!

That's the starting point. After a few days of practising with counting backwards from 60, when you reach number 1 stay in your position with eyes closed. Breathe normally and enjoy the moment. Observe your thoughts like clouds moving in the sky pushed by the wind. Thoughts are coming and going. There is nothing more important at the moment. You are safe.

Breathe normally. Imagine one of your favourite colours. Feel it. That colour surrounds you, protects you, energises you. Stay inside that colour just for a while. Breathe normally. Before you open your eyes, just say thank you to yourself for that time again. You know that you are doing it because you love yourself. Feel that love! Open your eyes and stretch your body gently. Pay attention to your emotions, notice your feelings.

Check the time, BOOM! You did it, 5 minutes of meditation.

Step by step, you will build up: 5 minutes, 10 minutes, 15 minutes, 20 minutes of meditation time. You need it all. Every minute counts for feeling better and better results. If you need full voice guidelines, please find my recordings on YouTube – The Core Life Coaching.

FINAL NOTE

PLEASE CALM DOWN and LOVE YOURSELF!

For your own good, please calm down. High, negative emotions are not helping you at all. You are capable of managing your emotions. You have enormous power to control your emotions by training your brain to be quiet and calm because you are safe. Calming down is a skill. You can acquire this skill at any stage of Your life. It's entirely up to You. Your reward is self-love and happiness.

Use your brain, that's your tool number one! Learn more about your triggers, slow down and reflect on your feelings and release them, if they are not serving you. Learn from them and let them go, seek changes, replace them with new positive emotions.

Stay focused on only one goal. Your primary goal is to love yourself, to be happy, to be free. Make a clear action plan with baby steps to make small changes. Use all the tools above and try them truly or run detailed research online for more suitable exercises.

Finally, I believe in your willingness, your skills to transform your thoughts and emotions for your greatest good. If you need more guidelines, 1-to-1 sessions, contact me or find another practitioner.

Personally, I wish all my readers a happy journey towards a new, happy life. With my whole heart, I believe in you and your power to create your life. Love yourself today and be happy 5 seconds later.

With love,
Ewa

Acknowledgements

I am grateful to all mentors I have met on my way towards and during my transformation. My sincere apology to those who are not listed below. Although they still contributed to positive changes in so many lives with their willingness to share it with the rest of humanity.

Abraham Hicks – Ester Hicks
Louise Hay
Brene Brown
Mel Robbins
Dr Bruce Lipton
Bob Baker
Peter Sage
Dr Joe Dispenza

My endless gratitude to Ania Abczak, my sister from 'other' parents. Ania gave her heart, knowledge and tenacious work to make sure that every word in this book makes sense.

November 2022

EIN HERZ FÜR AUTOREN A HEART FOR AUTHORS À L'ÉCOUTE DES AUTEURS MIA ΚΑΡΔΙΑ ΓΙΑ ΣΥΓΓΡ
MÅ FOR FÖRFATTARE UN CORAZÓN POR LOS AUTORES YAZARLARIMIZA GÖNÜL VERELIM SZÍ
RE PER AUTORI ET HJERTE FOR FORFATTERE EEN HART VOOR SCHRIJVERS TEMOS OS AUTO
ZÖINKÉRT SERCE DLA AUTORÓW EIN HERZ FÜR AUTOREN A HEART FOR AUTHORS À L'ÉCOU
ŁAO ВСЕЙ ДУШОЙ К АВТОРАМ ETT HJÄRTA FÖR FÖRFATTARE À LA ESCUCHA DE LOS AUTOR
ΜΑΡΔΙΑ ΓΙΑ ΣΥΓΓΡΑΦΕΙΣ UN CUORE PER AUTORI ET HJERTE FOR FORFATTERE EEN
ARIMIZ RE ZÖINKÉRT SERCE DLA AUTORÓW EIN HERZ FÜR
SCHRIJ C CÃO ВСЕЙ ДУШОЙ К АВТОРАМ ETT HJÄRTA FÖ

The author

Ewa Babicka, an emigrant like many and a person like no other. She has been a family and a friend to so many, both relatives and those she met on her life's journey.

Ewa's unbreakable will and strength combined with an amazing, positive attitude and openness towards people equip her to help those less unfortunate. Working as a self-employed interpreter, and collaborating with organizations like the NHS allow Ewa to serve those in need.

With an arsenal of empathy, optimism and energy she supports not only those she works with but also those around her.

Ewa loves people and cares about their well-being which is why she continues to educate herself in many directions such as CBT, life coaching and mediation.

For Ewa the zest of life does not ware off, and that self-improvement and appreciation for others is worth investing in.

Ewa's love for nature, physical activity and personal reflection enable her to keep an inner balance.

The publisher

He who stops getting better stops being good.

This is the motto of novum publishing, and our focus is on finding new manuscripts, publishing them and offering long-term support to the authors.
Our publishing house was founded in 1997, and since then it has become THE expert for new authors and has won numerous awards.

Our editorial team will peruse each manuscript within a few weeks free of charge and without obligation.

You will find more information about novum publishing and our books on the internet:

www.novum-publishing.co.uk